HARPER'S SCIENTIFIC MEMOIRS

EDITED BY

J. S. AMES, Ph.D.

PROFESSOR OF PHYSICS IN JOHNS HOPKINS UNIVERSITY

III.

RÖNTGEN RAYS

RÖNTGEN RAYS

MEMOIRS BY RÖNTGEN, STOKES
AND J. J. THOMSON

TRANSLATED AND EDITED BY

GEORGE F. BARKER, LL.D.

PROFESSOR OF PHYSICS IN THE UNIVERSITY OF PENNSYLVANIA

NEW YORK AND LONDON

HARPER & BROTHERS PUBLISHERS

1899

PREFACE

THE new kind of radiation known as X-rays, or Röntgen rays, from the name of their discoverer, were first observed and studied by Professor W. C. Röntgen, of the University of Würzburg, in 1895, and the announcement of their discovery was made in a paper which appeared that year, and which is reprinted in this volume. As was noticed later these radiations had been previously detected and some of their properties noted by other observers, notably Professor Lenard ; but it is to Röntgen that we owe the first systematic study of the methods of production and of the remarkable properties of these rays. Nearly all the general properties, both positive and negative, were investigated by Röntgen and carefully stated. These results are contained in the first three pages of this volume.

The most important experiments, however, and those which have led to the most important conclusions, were made by Professor J. J. Thomson, of Cambridge. They proved the fact that a dielectric traversed by these radiations became a conductor, or, in other words, was ionized. This discovery in the hands of Professor Thomson and his students has led to a series of most interesting and important researches, all bearing upon the intimate connection between matter and electricity.

Many hypotheses have been advanced to account for the peculiar properties of the X-rays. Röntgen himself at first was favorably inclined to the idea that they were waves due to longitudinal vibrations in the ether, but later he was convinced that they were essentially identical with light waves—that is,

v

with transverse waves in the ether.] There were grave obstacles, from many stand-points, to either of these theories, and the first suggestion which seemed to offer a satisfactory explanation of all the properties of the rays came when, instead of waves, the idea of pulses in the ether was introduced. This idea in its simplicity is that the cathode rays being negatively charged and travelling with great velocity, give rise to intensely sudden disturbances in the ether when their motions are stopped by reaching a solid obstacle. These disturbances are of the nature of irregular pulses, and their properties are quite different from those of regular trains of waves.

This idea of accounting for Röntgen rays by the theory of pulses occurred almost simultaneously to Sir George Gabriel Stokes, to Professor J. J. Thomson, and to Professor Lehmann, of Karlsruhe. Stokes's paper, in which he explains his theory, is reproduced in full in this volume, as are also the essential portions of Professor Thomson's article.

GENERAL CONTENTS

ON A NEW KIND OF RAYS

W. C. RÖNTGEN

———

Sitzungsberichte der Würzburger Physikalischen-Medicinischen Gesellschaft,
1895—Wiedemann, *Annalen der Physik und Chemie,* **64**, 1898

CONTENTS

ON A NEW KIND OF RAYS

W. C. RÖNTGEN

1. IF the discharge of a fairly large induction-coil be made to pass through a Hittorf vacuum-tube, or through a Lenard tube, a Crookes tube, or other similar apparatus, which has been sufficiently exhausted, the tube being covered with thin, black card-board which fits it with tolerable closeness, and if the whole apparatus be placed in a completely darkened room, there is observed at each discharge a bright illumination of a paper screen covered with barium platino-cyanide, placed in the vicinity of the induction-coil, the fluorescence thus produced being entirely independent of the fact whether the coated or the plain surface is turned towards the discharge-tube. This fluorescence is visible even when the paper screen is at a distance of two metres from the apparatus.

It is easy to prove that the cause of the fluorescence proceeds from the discharge-apparatus, and not from any other point in the conducting circuit.

2. The most striking feature of this phenomenon is the fact that an active agent here passes through a black card-board envelope, which is opaque to the visible and the ultra-violet rays of the sun or of the electric arc; an agent, too, which has the power of producing active fluorescence. Hence we may first investigate the question whether other bodies also possess this property.

We soon discover that all bodies are transparent to this agent,

3

though in very different degrees. I proceed to give a few examples : Paper is very transparent ;* behind a bound book of about one thousand pages I saw the fluorescent screen light up brightly, the printers' ink offering scarcely a noticeable hinderance. In the same way the fluorescence appeared behind a double pack of cards ; a single card held between the apparatus and the screen being almost unnoticeable to the eye. A single sheet of tin-foil is also scarcely perceptible ; it is only after several layers have been placed over one another that their shadow is distinctly seen on the screen. Thick blocks of wood are also transparent, pine boards two or three centimetres thick absorbing only slightly. A plate of aluminium about fifteen millimetres thick, though it enfeebled the action seriously, did not cause the fluorescence to disappear entirely. Sheets of hard rubber several centimetres thick still permit the rays to pass through them.† Glass plates of equal thickness behave quite differently, according as they contain lead (flint-glass) or not ; the former are much less transparent than the latter. If the hand be held between the discharge-tube and the screen, the darker shadow of the bones is seen within the slightly dark shadow-image of the hand itself. Water, carbon disulphide, and various other liquids, when they are examined in mica vessels, seem also to be transparent. That hydrogen is to any considerable degree more transparent than air I have not been able to discover. Behind plates of copper, silver, lead, gold, and platinum the fluorescence may still be recognized, though only if the thickness of the plates is not too great. Platinum of a thickness of 0.2 millimetre is still transparent ; the silver and copper plates may even be thicker. Lead of a thickness of 1.5 millimetres is practically opaque ; and on account of this property this metal is frequently most

* By "transparency" of a body I denote the relative brightness of a fluorescent screen placed close behind the body, referred to the brightness which the screen shows under the same circumstances, though without the interposition of the body.

† For brevity's sake I shall use the expression "rays"; and to distinguish them from others of this name I shall call them "X-rays." (See p. 11.)

useful. A rod of wood with a square cross-section (20 × 20 millimetres), one of whose sides is painted white with lead paint, behaves differently according as to how it is held between the apparatus and the screen. It is almost entirely without action when the X-rays pass through it parallel to the painted side; whereas the stick throws a dark shadow when the rays are made to traverse it perpendicular to the painted side. In a series similar to that of the metals themselves their salts can be arranged with reference to their transparency, either in the solid form or in solution.

√3. The experimental results which have now been given, as well as others, lead to the conclusion that the transparency of different substances, assumed to be of equal thickness, is essentially conditioned upon their density: no other property makes itself felt like this, certainly to so high a degree.

The following experiments show, however, that the density is not the only cause acting. I have examined, with reference to their transparency, plates of glass, aluminium, calcite, and quartz, of nearly the same thickness; and while these substances are almost equal in density, yet it was quite evident that the calcite was sensibly less transparent than the other substances, which appeared almost exactly alike. No particularly strong fluorescence (see p. 6 below) of calcite, especially by comparison with glass, has been noticed.

4. All substances with increase in thickness become less transparent. In order to find a possible relation between transparency and thickness, I have made .photographs (see p. 6 below) in which portions of the photographic plate were covered with layers of tin-foil, varying in the number of sheets superposed. Photometric measurements of these will be made when I am in possession of a suitable photometer.

5. Sheets of platinum, lead, zinc, and aluminium were rolled of such thickness that all appeared nearly equally transparent. The following table contains the absolute thickness of these sheets measured in millimetres, the relative thickness referred to that of the platinum sheet, and their densities:

Thickness	Relative Thickness	Density
Pt 0.018 mm.	1	21.5
Pb 0.05 "	3	11.3
Zn 0.10 "	6	7.1
Al 3.5 "	200	2.6

We may conclude from these values that different metals possess transparencies which are by no means equal, even when the product of thickness and density are the same. The transparency increases much more rapidly than this product decreases.

6. The fluorescence of barium platino-cyanide is not the only recognizable effect of the X-rays. It should be mentioned that other bodies also fluoresce; such, for instance, as the phosphorescent calcium compounds, then uranium glass, ordinary glass, calcite, rock-salt, and so on.

Of special significance in many respects is the fact that photographic dry plates are sensitive to the X-rays. We are, therefore, in a condition to determine more definitely many phenomena, and so the more easily to avoid deception; wherever it has been possible, therefore, I have controlled, by means of photography, every important observation which I have made with the eye by means of the fluorescent screen.

In these experiments the property of the rays to pass almost unhindered through thin sheets of wood, paper, and tin-foil is most important. The photographic impressions can be obtained in a non-darkened room with the photographic plates either in the holders or wrapped up in paper. On the other hand, from this property it results as a consequence that undeveloped plates cannot be left for a long time in the neighborhood of the discharge-tube, if they are protected merely by the usual covering of pasteboard and paper.

It appears questionable, however, whether the chemical action on the silver salts of the photographic plates is directly caused by the X-rays. It is possible that this action proceeds from the fluorescent light which, as noted above, is produced in the glass plate itself or perhaps in the layer of gelatin. "Films" can be used just as well as glass plates.

I have not yet been able to prove experimentally that the X-rays are able also to produce a heating action; yet we may well assume that this effect is present, since the capability of the X-rays to be transformed is proved by means of the observed fluoresence phenomena. It is certain, therefore, that all the X-rays which fall upon a substance do not leave it again as such.

The retina of the eye is not sensitive to these rays. Even if the eye is brought close to the discharge-tube, it observes nothing; although, as experiment has proved, the media contained in the eye must be sufficiently transparent to transmit the rays.

7. After I had recognized the transparency of various substances of relatively considerable thickness, I hastened to see how the X-rays behaved on passing through a prism, and to find whether they were thereby deviated or not.

Experiments with water and with carbon disulphide enclosed in mica prisms of about 30° refracting angle showed no deviation, either with the fluorescent screen or on the photographic plate. For purposes of comparison the deviation of rays of ordinary light under the same conditions was observed; and it was noted that in this case the deviated images fell on the plate about 10 or 20 millimetres distant from the direct image. By means of prisms made of hard rubber and of aluminium, also of about 30° refracting angle, I have obtained images on the photographic plate in which some small deviation may · perhaps be recognized. However, the fact is quite uncertain; the deviation, if it does exist, being so small that in any case the refractive index of the X-rays in the substances named cannot be more than 1.05 at the most. With a fluorescent screen I was also unable to observe any deviation.

Up to the present time experiments with prisms of denser metals have given no definite results, owing to their feeble transparency and the consequently diminished intensity of the transmitted rays.

7

With reference to the general conditions here involved on the one hand, and on the other to the importance of the question whether the X-rays can be refracted or not on passing from one medium into another, it is most fortunate that this subject may be investigated in still another way than with the aid of prisms. Finely divided bodies in sufficiently thick layers scatter the incident light and allow only a little of it to pass, owing to reflection and refraction; so that if powders are as transparent to X-rays as the same substances are in mass —equal amounts of material being presupposed—it follows at once that neither refraction nor regular reflection takes place to any sensible degree. Experiments were tried with finely powdered rock-salt, with fine electrolytic silver-powder, and with zinc-dust, such as is used in chemical investigations. In all these cases no difference was detected between the transparency of the powder and that of the substance in mass, either by observation with the fluorescent screen or with the photographic plate.

From what has now been said it is obvious that the X-rays cannot be concentrated by lenses; neither a large lens of hard rubber nor a glass lens having any influence upon them. The shadow-picture of a round rod is darker in the middle than at the edge; while the image of a tube which is filled with a substance more transparent than its own material is lighter at the middle than at the edge.

8. The question as to the reflection of the X-rays may be regarded as settled, by the experiments mentioned in the preceding paragraph, in favor of the view that no noticeable regular reflection of the rays takes place from any of the substances examined. Other experiments, which I here omit, lead to the same conclusion.

One observation in this connection should, however, be mentioned, as at first sight it seems to prove the opposite. I exposed to the X-rays a photographic plate which was protected from the light by black paper, and the glass side of which was turned towards the discharge-tube giving the X-rays. The sensitive film was covered, for the most part, with polished plates of platinum, lead, zinc, and aluminium arranged in the form of a star. On the developed negative it was seen plainly that the darkening under the platinum, the lead, and particularly the zinc, was stronger than under the other plates, the aluminium having exerted no action at all. It appears, therefore, that these three metals reflect the rays. Since, however, other explanations of the stronger darkening are conceivable, in a second experiment, in order to be sure, I placed between the sensitive film and the metal plates a piece of thin aluminium-foil, which is opaque to ultra-violet rays, but is very transparent to the X-rays. Since the same result substantially was again obtained, the reflection of X-rays from the metals above named is proved.

If we compare this fact with the observation already mentioned that powders are as transparent as coherent masses, and with the further fact that bodies with rough surfaces behave like polished bodies with reference to the passage of the X-rays, as shown also in the last experiment, we are led to the conclusion already stated that regular reflection does not take place, but that bodies behave towards the X-rays as turbid media do towards light.

Since, moreover, I could detect no evidence of refraction of these rays in passing from one medium into another, it would seem that X-rays move with the same velocity in all substances; and, further, that this speed is the same in the medium which is present everywhere in space and in which the particles of matter are imbedded. These particles hinder the propagation of the X-rays, the effect being greater, in general, the more dense the substance concerned.

9. Accordingly it might be possible that the arrangement of particles in the substance exercised an influence on its transparency; that, for instance, a piece of calcite might be transparent in different degrees for the same thickness, according as it is traversed in the direction of the axis, or at right angles to it. Experiments, however, on calcite and quartz gave a negative result.

10. It is well known that Lenard came to the conclusion,

from the results of his beautiful experiments on the transmission of the cathode rays of Hittorf through a thin sheet of aluminium, that these rays are phenomena of the ether, and that they diffuse themselves through all bodies. We can say the same of our rays.

In his most recent research, Lenard has determined the absorptive power of different substances for the cathode rays, and, among others, has measured it for air from atmospheric pressure to 4.10, 3.40, 3.10, referred to 1 centimetre, according to the rarefaction of the gas contained in the discharge-apparatus. Judging from the discharge - pressure as estimated from the sparking distance, I have had to do in my experiments for the most part with rarefactions of the same order of magnitude, and only rarely with less or greater ones. I have succeeded in comparing by means of the L. Weber photometer—I do not possess a better one—the intensities, taken in atmospheric air, of the fluorescence of my screen at two distances from the discharge-apparatus—about 100 and 200 millimetres; and I have found from three experiments, which agree very well with each other, that the intensities vary inversely as the squares of the distances of the screen from the discharge-apparatus. Accordingly, air absorbs a far smaller fraction of the X-rays than of the cathode rays. This result is in entire agreement with the observation mentioned above, that it is still possible to detect the fluorescent light at a distance of 2 metres from the discharge-apparatus.

Other substances behave in general like air; they are more transparent to X-rays than to cathode rays.

11. A further difference, and a most important one, between the behavior of cathode rays and of X-rays lies in the fact that I have not succeeded, in spite of many attempts, in obtaining a deflection of the X-rays by a magnet, even in very intense fields.

The possibility of deflection by a magnet has, up to the present time, served as a characteristic property of the cathode rays; although it was observed by Hertz and Lenard that there are different sorts of cathode rays, " which are distinguished from each other by their production of phosphorescence, by the amount of their absorption, and by the extent of their deflection by a magnet." A considerable deflection, however, was noted in all of the cases investigated by them; so that I do not think that this characteristic will be given up except for stringent reasons.

12. According to experiments especially designed to test the question, it is certain that the spot on the wall of the discharge-tube which fluoresces the strongest is to be considered as the main centre from which the X-rays radiate in all directions. The X-rays proceed from that spot where, according to the data obtained by different investigators, the cathode rays strike the glass wall. If the cathode rays within the discharge-apparatus are deflected by means of a magnet, it is observed that the X-rays proceed from another spot—namely, from that which is the new terminus of the cathode rays.

For this reason, therefore, the X-rays, which it is impossible to deflect, cannot be cathode rays simply transmitted or reflected without change by the glass wall. The greater density of the gas outside of the discharge-tube certainly cannot account for the great difference in the deflection, according to Lenard.

I therefore reach the conclusion that the X-rays are not identical with the cathode rays, but that they are produced by the cathode rays at the glass wall of the discharge-apparatus.

13. This production does not take place in glass alone, but, as I have been able to observe in an apparatus closed by a plate of aluminium 2 millimetres thick, in this metal also. Other substances are to be examined later.

14. The justification for calling by the name "rays" the agent which proceeds from the wall of the discharge-apparatus I derive in part from the entirely regular formation of shadows, which are seen when more or less transparent bodies are brought between the apparatus and the fluorescent screen (or the photographic plate).

I have observed, and in part photographed, many shadow-pictures of this kind, the production of which has a particular charm. I possess, for instance, photographs of the shadow of the profile of a door which separates the rooms in which, on one side, the discharge-apparatus was placed, on the other the photographic plate; the shadow of the bones of the hand; the shadow of a covered wire wrapped on a wooden spool; of a set of weights enclosed in a box; of a galvanometer in which the magnetic needle is entirely enclosed by metal; of a piece of metal whose lack of homogeneity becomes noticeable by means of the X-rays, etc.

Another conclusive proof of the rectilinear propagation of the X-rays is a pin-hole photograph which I was able to make of the discharge-apparatus while it was enveloped in black paper; the picture is weak but unmistakably correct.

15. I have tried in many ways to detect interference phenomena of the X-rays; but, unfortunately, without success, perhaps only because of their feeble intensity.

16. Experiments have been begun, but are not yet finished, to ascertain whether electrostatic forces affect the X-rays in any way.

17. In considering the question what are the X-rays—which, as we have seen, cannot be cathode rays—we may perhaps at first be led to think of them as ultra-violet light, owing to their active fluorescence and their chemical actions. But in so doing we find ourselves opposed by the most weighty considerations. If the X-rays are ultra-violet light, this light must have the following properties:

(*a*) On passing from air into water, carbon disulphide, aluminium, rock-salt, glass, zinc, etc., it suffers no noticeable refraction.

(*b*) By none of the bodies named can it be regularly reflected to any appreciable extent.

(*c*) It cannot be polarized by any of the ordinary methods.

(*d*) Its absorption is influenced by no other property of substances so much as by their density.

That is to say, we must assume that these ultra-violet rays behave entirely differently from the ultra-red, visible, and ultra-violet rays which have been known up to this time.

I have been unable to come to this conclusion, and so have sought for another explanation.

There seems to exist some kind of relationship between the new rays and light rays; at least this is indicated by the formation of shadows, the fluorescence and the chemical action produced by them both. Now, we have known for a long time, that there can be in the ether longitudinal vibrations besides the transverse light-vibrations; and, according to the views of different physicists, these vibrations must exist. Their existence, it is true, has not been proved up to the present, and consequently their properties have not been investigated by experiment.

Ought not, therefore, the new rays to be ascribed to longitudinal vibrations in the ether?

I must confess that in the course of the investigation I have become more and more confident of the correctness of this idea, and so, therefore, permit myself to announce this conjecture, although I am perfectly aware that the explanation given still needs further confirmation.

WÜRZBURG, Physikalisches Institut der Universität.

December, 1895.

SECOND COMMUNICATION

Since my work must be interrupted for several weeks, I take the opportunity of presenting in the following paper some new phenomena which I have observed.

18. It was known to me at the time of my first publication that X-rays can discharge electrified bodies; and I conjecture that in Lenard's experiments it was the X-rays, and not the cathode rays, which had passed unchanged through the aluminium window of his apparatus, which produced the action described by him upon electrified bodies at a distance. I have, however, delayed the publication of my experiments until I could contribute results which are free from criticism.

These results can be obtained only when the observations are made in a space which is protected completely, not only from

13

the electrostatic forces proceeding from the vacuum-tube, from the conducting wires, from the induction apparatus, etc., but is also closed against air which comes from the neighborhood of the discharge-apparatus.

To secure these conditions I had a chamber made of zinc plates soldered together, which was large enough to contain myself and the necessary apparatus, which could be closed air-tight, and which was provided with an opening which could be closed by a zinc door. The wall opposite the door was for the most part covered with lead. At a place near the dis-charge-apparatus, which was set up outside the case, the zinc wall, together with the lining of sheet-lead, was cut out for a width of 4 centimetres; and the opening was covered again air-tight with a thin sheet of aluminium. The X-rays penetrated through this window into the observation space.

I observed the following phenomena :

(a) Electrified bodies in air, charged either positively or negatively, are discharged if X-rays fall upon them; and this process goes on the more rapidly the more intense the rays are. The intensity of the rays was estimated by their action on a fluorescent screen or a photographic plate.

It is immaterial in general whether the electrified bodies are conductors or insulators. Up to the present I have not found any specific difference in the behavior of different bodies with reference to the rate of discharge; nor as to the behavior of positive and negative electricity. Yet it is not impossible that small differences may exist.

(b) If the electrified conductor be surrounded not by air but by a solid insulator, e. g. paraffin, the radiation has the same action as would result from exposure of the insulating envelope to a flame connected to the earth.

(c) If this insulating envelope be surrounded by a close-fitting conductor which is connected to the earth, and which, like the insulator, is transparent to X-rays, the radiation produces on the inner electrified conductor no action which can be detected by my apparatus.

(d) The observations noted under (a), (b), (c) indicate that

14

air through which X-rays have passed possesses the power of discharging electrified bodies with which it comes in contact.

(e) If this is really the case, and if, further, the air retains this property for some time after it has been exposed to the X-rays, then it must be possible to discharge electrified bodies which have not been themselves exposed to the rays, by conducting to them air which has thus been exposed.

We may convince ourselves in various ways that this conclusion is correct. One method of experiment, although perhaps not the simplest, I shall describe.

I used a brass tube 3 centimetres wide and 45 centimetres long; at a distance of some centimetres from one end a part of the wall of the tube was cut away and replaced by a thin aluminium plate; at the other end, through an air-tight cap, a brass ball fastened to a metal rod was introduced into the tube in such a manner as to be insulated. Between the ball and the closed end of the tube there was soldered a side-tube which could be connected with an exhaust-apparatus; so that when this is in action the brass ball is subjected to a stream of air which on its way through the tube has passed by the aluminium window. The distance from the window to the ball was over 20 centimetres.

I arranged this tube inside the zinc chamber in such a position that the X-rays could enter through the aluminium window of the tube perpendicular to its axis. The insulated ball lay then in the shadow, out of the range of the action of these rays. The tube and the zinc case were connected by a conductor, the ball was joined to a Hankel electroscope.

It was now observed that a charge (either positive or negative) given to the ball was not influenced by the X-rays so long as the air remained at rest in the tube, but that the charge instantly decreased considerably if by exhaustion the air which had been subjected to the rays was drawn past the ball. If by means of storage cells the ball was maintained at a constant potential, and if the modified air was drawn continuously through the tube, an electric current arose just as if

15

the ball were connected to the wall of the tube by a poor conductor.

(*f*) The question arises, How does the air lose the property which is given it by the X-rays? It is not yet settled whether it loses this property gradually of itself—*i. e.*, without coming in contact with other bodies. On the other hand, it is certain that a brief contact with a body of large surface, which does not need to be electrified, can make the air inactive. For instance, if a thick enough stopper of wadding is pushed into the tube so far that the modified air must pass through it before it reaches the electrified ball, the charge on the ball remains unaffected even while the exhaustion is taking place.

If the wad is in front of the aluminium window, the result obtained is the same as it would be without the wad; a proof that it is not particles of dust which are the cause of the observed discharge.

Wire gratings act like wadding; but the gratings must be very fine, and many layers must be placed over each other if the modified air is to be inactive after it is drawn through them. If these gratings are not connected to the earth, as has been assumed, but are connected to a source of electricity at a constant potential, I have always observed exactly what I had expected; but these experiments are not yet completed.

(*g*) If the electrified bodies, instead of being in air, are placed in dry hydrogen, they are also discharged by the X-rays. The discharge in hydrogen seemed to me to proceed somewhat more slowly; yet this is still uncertain on account of the difficulty of obtaining exactly equal intensities of the X-rays in consecutive experiments.

The method of filling the apparatus with hydrogen precludes the possibility that the layer of air which was originally present, condensed on the surface of the bodies, played any important rôle.

(*h*) In spaces which are highly exhausted the discharge of a body by the direct incidence of X-rays proceeds much more slowly—in one case about seventy times more slowly—than in

16

the same vessels when filled with air or hydrogen at atmospheric pressure.

(*i*) Experiments are about to be begun on the behavior of a mixture of chlorine and hydrogen under the influence of X-rays.

(*j*) In conclusion I would like to mention that the results of investigations on the discharging action of X-rays in which the influence of the surrounding gas is not taken into account should be received with great caution.

19. It is advantageous in many cases to include a Tesla apparatus (condenser and transformer) between the discharge-apparatus which furnishes the X-rays and the induction-coil. This arrangement has the following advantages: first, the discharge-apparatus is less easily penetrated and is less heated; second, the vacuum maintains itself for a longer time, at least in my self-constructed apparatus; third, many discharge-tubes under these conditions give more intense X-rays. With tubes which have not been exhausted sufficiently or have been exhausted too much to be driven satisfactorily by the induction-coil alone, the addition of the Tesla transformer renders good service.

The question immediately arises—and I allow myself to mention it without being able to contribute anything to its solution at present—whether X-rays can be produced by a continuous discharge under constant difference of potential; or whether variations of this potential are essential and necessary for the production of the rays.

20. In paragraph 13 of my first memoir I announced that X-rays could originate not only in glass, but in aluminium also. In the continuation of my experiments in this direction I have not found any solid body which cannot, under the action of the cathode rays, produce X-rays. There is also no reason known to me why liquids and gases may not behave in the same manner.

Quantitative differences in the behavior of different substances have appeared, however. If, for instance, the cathode rays fall upon a plate one half of which is made of platinum 0.3

millimetre thick, the other half of aluminium 1 millimetre thick, we see on the photographic image of this double plate, taken by means of a pin-hole camera, that the platinum sends out many more X-rays from the side struck by the cathode rays (the front side) than does the aluminium from the same side. However, from the rear side the platinum emits practically no X-rays, while the aluminium sends out relatively many. These last rays are produced in the front layers of the aluminium and pass through the plate.

We can easily devise an explanation of this observation, yet it may be advisable to learn other properties of the X-rays before so doing.

It must be mentioned, however, that there is a practical importance in the facts observed. For the production of the most intense X-rays platinum is best suited, according to my experiments up to the present. I have used for some weeks with great success a discharge-apparatus in which the cathode is a concave mirror of aluminium, and the anode is a plate of platinum placed at the centre of curvature of the mirror and inclined to the axis of the mirror at an angle of 45°.

21. The X-rays proceed in this case from the anode. I must conclude, though, from experiments with apparatus of different kinds that it is entirely immaterial, so far as the intensity of the X-rays is concerned, whether the place where the rays are produced is the anode or not.

A discharge-apparatus was prepared specially for experiments with the alternating currents of the Tesla transformer; in it both electrodes were aluminium concave mirrors whose axes were at right angles; at their common centre of curvature there was placed a platinum plate to receive the cathode rays. Further information will be given later as to the usefulness of this apparatus.

WÜRZBURG, Physikalisches Institut der Universität.

March 9, 1896.

18

\

FURTHER OBSERVATIONS ON THE PROP-ERTIES OF THE X-RAYS

BY

W. C. RÖNTGEN

———

THIRD COMMUNICATION

Sitzungsbericht der Königlichen preussischen Akademie der Wissenschaften zu Berlin, 1897—Wiedemann, *Annalen der Physik und der Chemie*, **64**, 1898.

CONTENTS

FURTHER OBSERVATIONS ON THE PROPERTIES OF THE X-RAYS

BY

W. C. RÖNTGEN

THIRD COMMUNICATION

1. If an opaque plate be placed between a discharge-apparatus* which is emitting intense X-rays and a fluorescent screen, in such a position that it shades the entire screen, there may still be noticed, in spite of the plate, an illumination of the barium platino-cyanide. This illumination can be seen even when the screen lies directly on the plate; and one is inclined at first sight to consider the plate as transparent. If, however, the screen lying on the plate be covered by a thick pane of glass, the fluorescent light becomes much weaker; and it vanishes entirely if, instead of using a glass plate, the screen is surrounded by a cylinder of sheet-lead 0.1 centimetre thick, which is closed at one end by the non-transparent plate, and at the other by the head of the observer.

The phenomenon now described may be due either to diffraction of rays of very great wave-length, or to the fact that the bodies which surround the discharge-apparatus and through which the rays pass, especially the air, themselves emit X-rays.

* All the discharge-tubes mentioned in the following communication are constructed according to the principle given in paragraph 20 of my second paper. The greater portion of them I obtained from the firm of Greiner & Friedrichs, in Stutzerbach i. Th., whom I wish to thank publicly for the material which has been furnished me in such abundance and without expense.

21

The latter explanation is the correct one, as may be proved with the following apparatus, among others : The figure represents a very thick-walled glass bell-jar, 20 centimetres high and 10 centimetres broad, which is closed by a thick zinc plate

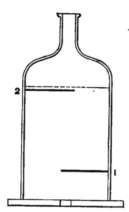

cemented on. At 1 and 2 are inserted plates of lead in the shape of circular segments; these are somewhat larger than half the cross-section of the jar, and prevent the X-rays, which enter through an opening in the zinc plate covered with a celluloid film, from reaching directly the space above the lead plate, 2. On the upper side of this sheet of lead there is fastened a small barium platino-cyanide screen, which nearly fills the entire cross-section of the jar. This cannot be struck either by the direct rays or by such as have suffered a single diffuse reflection at a solid body (e. g., the glass wall). The jar is filled with dust-free air before each experiment. If X-rays are made to enter the jar in such a manner that they are all received upon the lead screen 1, no fluorescence is observed at 2 ; the fluorescent screen first begins to light up on the half not covered by the lead plate 2 only when by tipping the bell-jar direct radiation reaches the space between 1 and 2. If the bell-jar is now connected to an aspirator-pump worked by a stream of water, it is observed that the fluorescence becomes more and more weak as the exhaustion proceeds ; but when the air is readmitted the intensity again increases.

Since now, as I have found, the mere contact with air which has been exposed shortly before to X-rays does not produce any sensible fluorescence of the barium platino-cyanide, we must conclude from the experiment described that air during its exposure to radiation emits X-rays in all directions.

If our eyes were as sensitive to X-rays as they are to light-rays, a discharge-apparatus in operation would appear to us like a light burning in a room moderately filled with tobacco smoke ; perhaps the colors of the direct rays and of those coming from the particles of air might be different.

The question as to whether the rays emitted by a body which is receiving radiation are of the same kind as those which are incident, or, in other words, whether the cause of these rays is diffuse reflection or a process like fluorescence, I have not yet been able to decide. The fact that the rays coming from the air are photographically active can be proved easily ; and this action makes itself noticeable sometimes in a way not desired by the observer. In order to guard against this action, as is often necessary in long exposures, the photographic plates must be protected by suitable lead casings.

2. In order to compare the intensity of the radiation of two discharge - tubes, and for various other experiments, I have used an arrangement which is based on the principle of the Bouguer photometer, and which, for the sake of simplicity, I shall call a photometer also. A rectangular sheet of lead 35 centimetres high, 150 centimetres long, and 0.15 centimetre thick, supported on a board frame, is placed vertically in the middle of a long table. At each side of this is placed a discharge-tube, which can be moved along the table. At one end of the lead strip a fluorescent screen* is so placed that each half receives radiation perpendicularly from one tube only. In effecting the measurements, adjustments are made until there is equal brightness of the fluorescence on the two halves.

Some remarks on the use of this instrument may find a place here. It should be mentioned first that the settings are often made more difficult by the lack of constancy of the source of radiation, the tubes responding to every irregularity in the interruption of the primary current, such as occur with the

* In this and other experiments the Edison fluorescent screen has proved most useful. This consists of a box like a stereoscope which can be held light-tight against the head of the observer, and whose card-board end is covered with barium platino-cyanide. Edison uses tungstate of calcium in place of barium platino-cyanide ; but I prefer the latter for many reasons.

Deprez interrupter, and especially with the Foucault instrument. Repeated settings are therefore advisable. In the second place, I should here enumerate the conditions which influence the brightness of a given fluorescent screen struck by X-rays in such rapid succession that the eye of the observer can no longer detect the intermittence of the radiation. This brightness depends (1) upon the intensity of the radiation which proceeds from the platinum plate of the discharge-tube; (2) very probably upon the kind of rays striking the screen, since all kinds of rays (see below) are not necessarily equally active in producing fluorescence; (3) upon the distance of the screen from the centre of emission of the rays; (4) upon the absorption which the rays experience on their way to the barium platino-cyanide screen; (5) upon the number of discharges per second; (6) upon the duration of each single discharge; (7) upon the duration and the strength of the after-illumination of the barium platino-cyanide; and (8) upon the radiation falling on the screen from the bodies which surround the discharge-tube. In order to avoid errors, it must always be remembered that the conditions are in general like those which would exist if we had to compare, by means of fluorescent action, two intermittent sources of light of different colors, which are surrounded by an absorbing envelope placed in a turbid—or fluorescing—medium.

3. According to paragraph 12 of my first communication, the point in the discharge-apparatus which is struck by the cathode rays is the centre of emission of the X-rays, and from this these rays spread out "in all directions." It becomes now of interest to determine how the intensity of the radiation varies with the direction.

For this investigation the discharge-tubes best suited to the purpose are those in the shape of a sphere, with smoothly polished platinum plates, which are struck by the cathode rays at an angle of 45°. Even without further appliances we can recognize from the uniformly bright fluorescence of the hemispherical glass wall surrounding the platinum plate that very great differences of intensity in different directions do not exist; so that Lambert's law of emission does not hold in this case. Nevertheless, this fluorescence for the most part might still be due to the cathode rays.

To test this question more accurately, several tubes were examined by means of the photometer as to their radiation in different directions. Moreover, besides doing this, I have exposed with the same object photographic films bent into a semi-circle (radius 25 centimetres) about the platinum plate of the discharge-tube as a centre. In both experiments, however, the varying thickness of the different portions of the walls of the tube produced a disturbing action, because the X-rays, proceeding in different directions, were unequally absorbed. Yet by interposing thin plates of glass I finally succeeded in making the thickness of glass traversed about the same.

The result of these experiments is that the radiation through an imaginary hemisphere, described around the platinum plate as a centre, is nearly uniform almost out to the edge. It was not until the emission angle of the rays was about 80° that I noticed the beginning of a decrease in the radiation; and even then this decrease was relatively very small; so that the main change in the intensity occurs between 89° and 90°.

No difference in the kind of rays emitted at different angles have I been able to detect.

As a consequence of the distribution of intensity of the X-rays, as now described, the images of the platinum plate which are received—either on a fluorescent screen or on a photographic plate, through a pin-hole camera or with a narrow slit —must be more intense the greater the angle which the platinum plate makes with the screen or with the photographic plate; always presupposing that this angle does not exceed 80°. By means of suitable appliances which allow comparisons to be made between the images received simultaneously at different angles from the same discharge-tube, I have been able to confirm this conclusion.

A similar case of distribution of the intensity of emitted rays occurs in Optics in the case of fluorescence. If a few drops of fluorescein solution be allowed to fall into a rectangular tank

25

filled with water, and if at the same time we illuminate the
tank with white or with violet light, we observe that the
brightest fluorescence proceeds from the edges of the threads
of the slowly sinking fluorescein—*i. e.*, from the places where
the emission angle of the fluorescent light is the greatest. As
Stokes has remarked, *à propos* of a similar experiment, this
phenomenon is due to the fact that the rays which produce
fluorescence are absorbed by the fluorescein solution much
more strongly than is the fluorescent light itself. Now it is
worthy of note that the cathode rays, which produce the
X - rays, are absorbed by platinum much more than are the
X-rays, and it is easy to conjecture from this that a relationship exists between the two phenomena—the transformation of
ordinary light into fluorescent light, and that of cathode rays
into X-rays. A conclusive proof, of any kind, of such an assumption is not known at the present time, however.

Moreover, with reference to the technique of the production
of shadow pictures by means of X-rays, the observations on the
distribution of intensity of the rays proceeding outward from
the platinum plate have a certain importance. According to
what has been stated above, it is advisable to place the discharge-tube in such a position that the rays used in producing
the image shall leave the platinum plate at as great an angle as
possible, though this should not be much over 80°. By this
means the sharpest pictures are produced ; and, if the platinum
plate be perfectly plane, and the construction of the tube of
such a kind that the oblique rays pass through a not materially
thicker glass wall than those rays which are emitted perpendicular to the platinum plate, then the radiation on the object
suffers no loss in intensity.

4. I have designated in my first communication by "transparency of a body" the ratio of the brightness of a fluorescent
screen placed perpendicular to the rays, and close behind the
body, to that which the screen shows when viewed under the
same conditions, but with the body removed. "Specific transparency" of a body will be used to indicate the transparency of
the body reduced to a thickness of unity ; this is equal to the

dth root of the transparency, if d is the thickness of the layer traversed, measured in the direction of the rays.

In order to determine the transparency, I have used principally, since my first communication, the photometer described above. The body to be investigated—aluminium, tin-foil, glass, etc., made in the form of a plate—was placed before one of the two equally bright fluorescent halves of the screen; and the inequality in brightness thus produced was made to vanish, either by increasing the distance of the radiating discharge-apparatus from the uncovered half of the screen, or by bringing the other tube nearer. In both cases the correctly measured ratio of the squares of the distances of the platinum plates of the discharge-tubes from the screen, before and after the displacement of the apparatus, is the desired value of the transparency of the interposed body. Both methods led to the same result. By the addition of a second plate to the first, the transparency of the second plate may be found in a similar manner for rays which have already passed through one.

The method above described presupposes that the brightness of a fluorescent screen varies inversely as the square of its distance from the source of rays, and this is true, in the first place, only if the air neither absorbs nor emits X-rays, and if, secondly, the brightness of the fluorescent light is proportional to the intensity of emission of rays of the same kind. The first condition is certainly not satisfied, and it is doubtful whether the second is; I convinced myself long ago by experiment, as already described in paragraph 10 of my first communication, that the deviations from the law of proportionality are so small that they can be safely neglected in the case before us. It should be mentioned with reference to the fact that X-rays also proceed from the irradiated body, first, that a difference in the transparency of a plate of aluminium 0.925 millimetre thick, and of 31 aluminium sheets laid upon one another, each of a thickness of 0.0299 millimetre—31 × 0.0299=0.927—could not be detected with the photometer used; and, second, that the brightness of the fluorescent screen was not sensibly different when the plate was close in front of the screen and when it was placed at a greater distance from it.

For aluminium, the results of this experiment on transparency are as follows :

TRANSPARENCY FOR PERPENDICULAR RAYS

	TUBE 2	TUBE 3	TUBE 4	TUBE 2
The first 1 mm. thick Al. plate	0.40	0.45	—	0.68
The second 1 mm. " " "	0.55	0.68	—	0.73
The first 2 mm. " " "	—	0.30	0.39	0.50
The second 2 mm. " " "	—	0.39	0.54	0.63

From these experiments, and from similar ones on glass and tin-foil, we deduce at once the following result : if we imagine a substance divided into layers of equal thickness, placed perpendicular to parallel rays, each of these layers is more transparent for the transmitted rays than the one before it ; or, in other words, the specific transparency of a substance increases with its thickness.

This result is completely in accord with what may be observed in the photograph of a tin-foil scale as described in paragraph 4 of my first communication ; and also with the fact that in photographic pictures the shadow of thin sheets—e. g., of the paper used to wrap up the plate—is proportionally strongly marked.

5. Even if two plates of different substances are equally transparent, this equality may not persist when the thickness of the plates is changed in the same ratio, nothing else being altered. This fact may be proved most easily by the help of two scales placed side by side ; for instance, one of platinum, the other of aluminium. I used for this purpose platinum-foil 0.0026 millimetre thick, and aluminium - foil 0.0299 millimetre thick. I brought the double scale before the fluorescent screen, or before a photographic plate, and allowed rays to fall upon it ; I found in one case that a single sheet of platinum was of equal transparency with a six-fold layer of aluminium ; but that the transparency of a double platinum layer was

equal not to that of a twelve-fold layer of aluminium, but to a sixteeen-fold layer. Using another discharge-tube, I obtained, 1 platinum = 8 aluminium ; 8 platinum = 90 aluminium. It follows from these experiments, therefore, that the ratio of the thickness of platinum and aluminium of equal transparency is smaller in proportion as the layers in question become thicker.

6. The ratio of the thicknesses of two equally transparent plates of different materials depends also upon the thickness and the material of the body—*e. g.*, the glass wall of the discharge-apparatus — which the rays must first traverse before they reach the plates in question.

In order to prove this conclusion—which is not surprising after what has been said in sections 4 and 5—we may use an arrangement which I call a platinum-aluminium window, and which, as we shall see, may also be used for other purposes. This consists of a rectangular piece (4.0 × 6.5 centimetres) of platinum-foil of 0.0026 millimetre thickness, which is cemented to a thin paper screen, and through which are punched 15 round holes, arranged in three rows, each hole having a diameter of 0.7 centimetre. These little windows are covered with panes of aluminium, 0.0299 millimetre thick, which fit exactly, and are carefully superposed in such a way that at the first window there is one disk ; at the second, two, etc. ; finally, at the fifteenth, fifteen disks. If this arrangement be brought in front of the fluorescent screen, it may be observed very plainly, in case the tubes are not too hard (see below), how many aluminium sheets have the same transparency as the platinum-foil. This number will be called the window-number.

For the window-number I obtained in one case by *direct* radiation the value 5. A plate of common soda-glass, 2 millimetres thick, was then held in front ; the window-number was 10. So that the ratio of the thickness of the platinum and aluminium sheets of equal transparency was reduced one-half when I used rays which had passed through a plate of glass 2 millimetres thick instead of using those coming direct from the discharge-apparatus. Q. E. D.

The following experiment also deserves mention in this

29

place : The platinum - aluminium window was laid upon a small package which contained 12 photographic films, and was then exposed; after development, the first film lying under the window showed the window-number 10, the twelfth the number 13 ; and the others, in proper order, the transition from 10 to 13.

7. The experiments communicated in sections 4, 5, and 6 refer to the modifications which the X-rays coming from a dis-charge-tube experience on passing through different substances. It will now be proved that one and the same substance, with the same thickness traversed, may be transparent in different degrees to rays which are emitted by different tubes.

In the following table are given, for this purpose, the values of the transparency of an aluminium plate 2 millimetres thick for rays produced in different tubes. Some of these values are taken from the first table on page 28 :

TRANSPARENCY FOR PERPENDICULAR RADIATION

	TUBES					
	1	2	3	4	2	5
of an Al. plate 2 mm. thick,	0.0044	0.22	0.30	0.39	0.50	0.59

The discharge - tubes are not materially different in their construction or in the thickness of their glass walls, but vary mainly in the degree of exhaustion of the contained gas and in the discharge - potential which is conditioned by this; tube 1 requires the lowest, tube 5 the highest, potential; or, as we shall say, to be brief, tube 1 is the "softest," tube 5 the "hardest." The same induction - coil — in direct connection with the tubes—the same interrupter, and the same strength of current in the primary were used in all the cases.

All the many other bodies which I have investigated behave in the same manner as aluminium; all are more transparent for the rays of a harder tube than for those of a softer one.*
This fact seems to me to be worthy of special consideration.

* See below for the behavior of " non-normal " tubes.

The ratio of the thicknesses of two equally transparent plates of different substances is also dependent upon the hardness of the tube used. This may be recognized immediately with the platinum-aluminium window (§ 5) ; with a very soft tube, for example, the window-number may be found to be 2 ; while with a tube which is very hard, but otherwise the same, the scale which reaches No. 15 does not extend far enough. This means, then, that the ratio of the thicknesses of platinum and aluminium of equal transparency is smaller in proportion as the tubes from which the rays come are harder, or—with reference to the result reported above—as the rays are less easily absorbed.

The different behavior of rays produced in tubes of different hardness is self-evident also in the familiar shadow-pictures of hands, etc. With a very soft tube, dark pictures are obtained in which the bones are not very prominent ; by using a harder tube the bones are very plain and all the details are visible, the soft parts, on the contrary, being weak ; while with an extremely hard tube only faint shadows are obtained, even of the bones. From what has been said it follows that the choice of the tube to be used must depend upon the constitution of the object to be pictured.

8. It still remains to note that the quality of the rays furnished by one and the same tube depends upon a variety of conditions. As the investigation made with the platinum-aluminium window shows, this is influenced : (1) By the manner and perfection with which the Deprez or Foucault interrupter* works—*i. e.*, by the variation of the primary current ; to this belongs the phenomenon so often observed, that single discharges out of a rapid succession produce X-rays which are not only particularly intense, but which are distinguished from the others by the [*slight*] extent to which they are absorbed ; (2) by a spark-gap which is included in the secondary circuit of the discharge-apparatus ; (3) by including in the circuit a Tesla

---

* A good Deprez interrupter works more regularly than a Foucault apparatus ; the latter, however, utilizes the primary current better.

transformer; (4) by the degree of exhaustion of the discharge-apparatus (as already mentioned); (5) by different conditions in the interior of the discharge-tube, which are not yet sufficiently understood. Several of these factors deserve a somewhat more extended consideration.

If we take a tube which has not yet been used, nor even exhausted, and connect it to the mercury-pump, we shall obtain, after the necessary pumping and heating, such a degree of exhaustion that the first X-rays are noticeable by means of the feeble illumination of the fluorescent screen lying near. A spark-gap in parallel with the tube gives sparks only a few millimetres long, the platinum-aluminium window shows only very low numbers, the rays are easily absorbed. The tube is "very soft." If now the spark-gap be put in series, or a Tesla transformer be inserted,* rays are emitted which are more intense and less easily absorbed. I found, for example, in one case, that by increasing the series spark-gap the window-number could be gradually brought from 2.5 to 10.

(These observations suggested the question whether at still higher pressures X-rays could not be obtained by the use of a Tesla transformer. This is, in fact, the case: using a narrow tube with wire-shaped electrodes, I could still observe X-rays when the pressure of the enclosed air amounted to 3.1 millimetres of mercury. If hydrogen were used instead of air, the pressure could be even higher. The lowest pressure at which X-rays can be produced in air I have not been able to determine; it is in many cases less than 0.0002 millimetre of mercury; so that the limits of pressure within which X-rays may arise are even now very considerable.)

Further exhaustion of a "very soft" tube — connected directly to the induction-coil—results in the radiation becoming more intense, and in a greater fraction of it passing through

* The fact that a spark-gap in series has the same effect as a Tesla transformer I was able to mention in the French edition of my second communication (*Arch. des Sci. Physique, etc., de Genève*, 1896); in the German publication this remark was omitted by accident.

the bodies on which it falls : a hand held in front of the fluorescent screen is more transparent than before, and the platinum-aluminium window gives a higher window-number. At the same time the spark-gap in parallel with the tube must be increased in length in order to send the discharge through the tube : the tube has become " harder." If the tube is exhausted still more, it becomes so " hard " that the spark-gap must be made more than 20 centimetres long ; and now the tube emits rays for which substances are unusually transparent : plates of iron 4 centimetres thick, for example, being seen to be transparent when viewed with the fluorescent screen.

The behavior, as now given, of a tube directly connected both with the pump and the induction-coil is the normal one ; but there often occur variations which are caused by the discharges themselves. The conduct of the tubes is in many cases quite unaccountable.

We have supposed the tube to become hard owing to continued exhaustion by the pump ; this may happen in another way. A fairly hard tube, sealed off from the pump, becomes of itself continually harder—unfortunately for the duration of its usefulness—even when it is used in the proper way for the production of X-rays ; that is to say, when discharges are sent through it which do not cause the platinum to glow, or at least only faintly. A gradual self-exhaustion takes place.

With such a tube, which has become hard in this way, I have obtained a most beautiful photographic shadow-picture of the double barrels of a hunting-rifle with cartridges in place, in which all the details of the cartridges, the internal faults of the damask barrels, etc., could be seen most distinctly and sharply. The distance from the platinum plate of the discharge-tube to the photographic plate was 15 centimetres, the time of exposure was 12 minutes — comparatively long owing to the small photographic action of these rays, which are less absorbable (see below). The Deprez interrupter must be replaced by the Foucault apparatus. It would be of interest to construct tubes which require still higher potentials to be used than has been possible up to the present time.

As to the cause of a tube's becoming hard when sealed off from the pump, the explanation given above is the self-exhaustion of the tube owing to the discharges. But this is not the only cause; there are also changes at the electrodes which influence the result. What they consist in I do not know.

A tube which has become too hard can be made softer by admission of air, often also by heating the tube or by reversing the direction of the current; or, finally, by sending powerful discharges through it. In the last case, however, the tube has acquired, for the most part, other properties than those mentioned above; thus it often requires, for instance, a very great discharge-potential, and yet furnishes rays which have a comparatively small window-number and which are easily absorbed. I need not continue further the discussion of the behavior of the "non-normal" tubes. The tubes constructed by Herr Zehnder, having a vacuum which can be regulated, since they contain a small piece of charcoal, have done me very good service.

The observations communicated in this section, and others also, have led me to the opinion that the composition of the rays emitted from a discharge-tube provided with a platinum anode is conditioned essentially upon the duration of the discharge-current. The degree of exhaustion, the hardness, play a part only because of this, since the form of the discharge depends upon it. If we can produce in any way whatever the form of discharge necessary for the appearance of the X-rays, X-rays can be produced, and this even at relatively high pressures.

In conclusion, it is worth mentioning that the quality of the rays produced by a tube is not changed, or, at most, only very slightly, by very considerable changes in the strength of the primary current, it being presupposed that the interrupter works the same in all cases. The intensity of the X-rays, on the contrary, is proportional within certain limits to the strength of the primary current, as the following experiment shows: The distances from the discharge-apparatus at which, in a certain case, the fluorescence of the barium platino-cyanide screen was just noticeable amounted to 18.1 millimetres, 25.7 millimetres, and 37.5 millimetres, when the strength of the primary current was increased from 8 to 16 to 32 amperes. The squares of the distances are in nearly the same ratio as the corresponding current-strengths.

9. The results stated in the last five paragraphs were derived immediately from the individual experiments mentioned. If we review the whole of these individual results, we reach the following conclusions, being led to them in part by the analogy which exists between the behavior of optical rays and X-rays :

(*a*) The rays emitted by a discharge - apparatus consist of a mixture of rays which are absorbed in different degrees and which have different intensities.

(*b*) The composition of this mixture of rays depends essentially upon the duration of the discharge-current.

(*c*) The rays selected for absorption by various substances are different for the different bodies.

(*d*) Since the X-rays are generated by the cathode rays, and since both have properties in common—production of fluorescence, photographic and electrical action, and absorbability, the amount of which is essentially conditioned upon the density of the medium through which the radiation passes, etc.—the hypothesis at once suggests itself that both phenomena are of the same nature. Without wishing to bind myself unconditionally to this view, I may remark that the results of the last few paragraphs are calculated to resolve a difficulty which has existed in connection with this hypothesis up to the present. This difficulty arises, first, from the great difference between the absorption of the cathode rays investigated by Herr Lenard and that of the X-rays ; and, second, from the fact that the transparency of bodies for these cathode rays depends upon a different law of the densities of the bodies from that governing the transparency for the X-rays.

As to the first difficulty, two points should be mentioned : (1) We have seen in § 7 that there are X-rays whose absorptions are very different ; and we know from the investigations of Hertz and Lenard that the different cathode rays also differ from each other with reference to their absorption. Even if we admit, therefore, that the softest tube mentioned on p. 30 furnishes X-rays whose absorption is far less than that of the cathode rays investigated by Herr Lenard, yet we cannot doubt that there are X-rays which are absorbed more, and, on the other hand, cathode rays which are absorbed less even than those. It therefore seems perfectly possible that by further experiments rays will be found which form, so far as absorption is concerned, the link between the one kind of rays and the other. (2) We found in § 4 that the specific transparency of a body is smaller in proportion as the plate traversed is thinner. Consequently, if in our experiments we had taken plates as thin as those of Herr Lenard, we might have obtained values for the absorption of the X-rays which would approximate more closely those of Lenard.

With reference to the varying influence of the density of bodies on their absorption of X-rays and of cathode rays, it should be said that this difference is found to be smaller in proportion as more strongly absorbable X-rays are chosen for the experiment (§ 7 and § 8), and in proportion as the plates traversed are made thinner (§ 5). Consequently, one must acknowledge the possibility that this difference in the behavior of the two kinds of rays may, by means of further experiments, be made to vanish at the same time as the differences mentioned above.

With reference to this absorbability, the rays which come nearest to each other are the cathode rays which are especially present in very hard tubes and the X-rays which are emitted from the platinum plate in very soft tubes.

10. Besides exciting fluorescence, the X-rays have, as is well known, photographic, electric, and other actions; and it is of interest to know how far these continue parallel with each other as the source of radiation is altered. I have been obliged to confine myself to comparing the two actions first named.

The platinum-aluminium window is suited for this work also. One of these is placed upon a photographic plate which is wrapped up, a second is brought in front of the fluorescent screen, and both are then placed at equal distances from the discharge-apparatus. The X-rays had exactly the same media to traverse in order to reach the sensitive layer of the photographic plate and the barium platino-cyanide. During the exposure I observed the screen and determined the window-number; after development, the window-number was also determined upon the photographic plate; and then both numbers were compared. The result of these experiments is that, using softer tubes (window-numbers 4–7), no difference could be observed; but when harder tubes were used it seemed to me that the window-number on the photographic plate was a little lower, at most one unit, than that determined by means of the fluorescent screen. This observation, however, although repeatedly confirmed, is not quite free from criticism, because the determination of the high window-numbers at the fluorescent screen is quite uncertain.

The following result is, however, entirely certain. If we arrange, with the photometer described in § 2, a hard and a soft tube so as to have the same brightness at the fluorescent screen, and if a photographic plate is substituted for the screen, we see after development of this plate that the half of the plate which received the rays from the hard tube is considerably less blackened than the other. The radiations which produce equal intensities of fluorescence have different photographic actions.

In considering this result we must not leave out of account the fact that neither the fluorescent screen nor the photographic plate uses up completely the incident rays; both transmit many rays which can again produce fluorescent or photographic action. The result communicated holds true, therefore, only for the thickness of the sensitive photographic film employed and the layer of barium platino-cyanide accompanying it.

How very transparent to the X-rays from tubes of average hardness the sensitive film of the photographic plate is is shown by an experiment with 96 "films" laid one over another, 25 centimetres distant from the source of radiation, exposed for 5 minutes, and protected against the radiation of the air by an envelope of lead. Even on the last one a photographic action can be recognized plainly, while the first is scarcely over-exposed. Induced by this and similar observations, I have inquired of several firms who furnish photographic plates whether it would not be possible to prepare plates which were more suited for photography with X-rays than the ordinary ones. The samples forwarded were not, however, serviceable.

I have had many opportunities, as mentioned already on p. 31, to perceive that very hard tubes, under otherwise equal circumstances, require a longer time of exposure than those moderately hard; this is easily understood if we remember the result communicated in § 9, according to which all bodies so far examined are more transparent for rays which are emitted by hard tubes than for those coming from soft ones. The fact that with very soft tubes the exposure must again be long is explained by the lack of intensity of the rays emitted by them.

If the intensity of the rays is increased by increasing the primary current (see p. 31), the photographic action is increased in the same degree as the intensity of the fluorescence; and in this case, as also in that mentioned above where the intensity of the radiation on the fluorescent screen is altered by changing the distance of the screen from the source of the rays, the brightness of the fluorescence is proportional, or at least nearly so, to the intensity of the radiation. This law cannot, however, be applied generally.

11. In conclusion, I beg the privilege of mentioning the following isolated points:

In a discharge-tube properly made and not too soft, the X-rays come mainly from a spot on the platinum plate struck by the cathode rays, which is from 1 to 2 millimetres in size. But this is not the only starting-point: the whole plate and a part of the wall of the tube emit rays, although to a very small extent. Cathode rays proceed from the cathode in all directions; their intensity, however, is important only in the neighborhood of the axis of the concave mirror; and therefore the most intense X-rays originate on the platinum plate at the point where this axis meets it. If the tube is very hard and the platinum

38

thin, a great many X-rays are emitted from the rear side of the platinum plate, and, as is shown by a pin-hole camera, from a point which also lies on the axis of the mirror.

In these hardest tubes, also, the maximum of intensity of the cathode rays can be deflected from the platinum plate by means of a magnet. Some experiments on soft tubes led me to take up again, with better apparatus, the question of the possibility of magnetic deflection of X-rays; I hope to be able to communicate soon the results of these experiments.

The experiments mentioned in my first communication on the transparency of plates of the same thickness which are cut from a crystal according to different directions have been continued. I have investigated plates of calcite, quartz, tourmaline, beryl, aragonite, apatite, and barite. No influence of direction on the transparency could be detected even with the improved apparatus.

The fact observed by Herr G. Brandes, that the X-rays can produce a light-sensation in the retina of the eye, I have found confirmed. There stands also in my observation-journal a note at the beginning of the month of November, 1895, according to which I perceived a feeble light-sensation, which spread over the whole field of vision, when I was in an entirely darkened room near a wooden door on the other side of which there was a Hittorf tube, whenever discharges were sent through the tube. Since I observed this phenomenon only once, I thought it a subjective one, and the fact that I never saw it repeated is because, later, instead of the Hittorf tube, other apparatus was used, not exhausted so much, and not provided with platinum anodes. On account of their state of high exhaustion, Hittorf tubes furnish rays which are only slightly absorbed, and on account of the presence of a platinum anode, which is struck by the cathode rays, they furnish intense rays, a condition which is favorable for the production of the light-phenomenon referred to. I was obliged to replace the Hittorf tubes by others, because after a very short while all were perforated.

With the hard tubes now in general use the experiment of Brandes may be easily repeated. The following description of the mode of experimenting may be of some interest : If a vertical metal slit some tenths of a millimetre broad is held as close as possible before the open or closed eye, and if the head, completely enveloped in a black cloth, is then brought near the discharge apparatus, there is observed, after some practice, a weak, non-uniformly bright strip of light which, according to the place where the slit is in front of the eye, takes a different form—straight, curved, or circular. By a slow motion of the slit in a horizontal direction, these different forms can be made to pass gradually from one into the other. An explanation of the phenomenon is found immediately if we consider that the ball of the eye is cut by a lamellar sheaf of X-rays, and if we assume that the X-rays can excite fluorescence in the retina.

Since the beginning of my work on X-rays I have tried repeatedly to obtain diffraction phenomena with them; several times I have obtained with narrow slits, etc., phenomena whose appearance reminded one, it is true, of diffraction images ; but when by alteration of the conditions of experiment tests were made of the correctness of the explanation of these images by diffraction, it was refuted in every case ; and often I could prove directly that the phenomena had arisen in a way quite different from diffraction. I have no experiment to describe from which, with sufficient certainty, I could obtain proof of the existence of diffraction of the X-rays.

WÜRZBURG, Physikalisches Institut der Universität.

March 10, 1897.

WILHELM CONRAD RÖNTGEN was born March 27, 1845, in Lennep, Rhine Province, Germany, and is at the present time Professor of Physics at the University of Würzburg. He received his doctor's degree at Zürich in 1868, and became then an assistant to Kundt at Würzburg. He was finally appointed Professor of Physics at Giessen, from which university he was transferred to Würzburg. He has been engaged in many important researches which, in the main, have a bearing upon the connection between electricity and ordinary matter.

ON THE NATURE OF THE RÖNTGEN RAYS
(THE WILDE LECTURE)
BY
Sir G. G. STOKES, Bart., M.A., LL.D., F.R.S.

(*Memoirs and Proceedings of the Manchester Literary and Philosophical Society*, **41**, Part IV., 1896-7.)

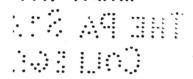

CONTENTS

ON THE NATURE OF THE RÖNTGEN RAYS
(THE WILDE LECTURE)
BY
SIR G. G. STOKES, BART., M.A., LL.D., F.R.S.

Delivered July 25, 1897.

EVER since the remarkable discovery of Professor Röntgen
was published, the subject has attracted a great deal of attention in all civilized countries, and numbers of physicists have
worked experimentally, endeavoring to make out the laws of
these rays, to determine their nature, if possible, and to arrange for their application. I am sorry to say that I have not
myself worked experimentally at the subject; and that being
the case, there is a certain amount of presumption, perhaps, in
my venturing to lecture on it. Still, I have followed pretty
well what has been done by others, and the subject borders
very closely on one to which I have paid considerable attention;
that is, the subject of light.

In Röntgen's original paper he stated that it was shown experimentally that the seat of these remarkable rays was the
place where the so-called cathodic rays fall on the opposite wall
of the highly exhausted tube in which they are produced. I
will not stop to describe what is meant by cathodic rays. It
would take me too much away from my subject, and I may
assume, I think, that the audience I am now addressing know
what is meant by that term. This statement of Röntgen's was
not, I think, universally accepted. Some experimentalists set
themselves to investigate the point by observing the positions
of the shadows cast by bodies subjected to the discharge of the
Röntgen rays—to investigate, I say, the place within the tube
from which the rays appeared to come. Now, when the shad-

ows were received on a photographic plate, and the shadow was joined to the substance casting the shadow, and the joining lines were produced backwards, as a rule they tended more or less nearly to meet somewhere within the tube—Crookes' tube, I will now call it—and some people seem to have had the idea that at that point of meeting or approximate meeting there was something going on which was the source of these rays. I have in my hands a paper published in St. Petersburg by Prince B. Galitzin and A. v. Karnojitzky, which contains some very elaborate photographs obtained in this way. A board was taken and ruled with cross lines at equal intervals, and at the points of intersection nails were struck in in an upright position. The board was placed on top of the photographic plate, with an opaque substance between—a substance which these strange Röntgen rays are capable of passing through, though it is impervious to light. The shadows cast by the nails were obtained on the photograph, and this paper contains a number of the photographs. It is remarkable, considering the somewhat large space in the tube over which the discharge from the cathode is spread, that the shadows are as sharp as they actually are; and the same thing may be affirmed of the ordinary shadows of the bones of the hand, for instance, which one so frequently sees now. Another remarkable point in these photographs is that in some cases it appears as if there were two shadows of the same nail, as though there were two different sources from which these strange rays come, both situated within the Crookes' tube. Now, have we a right to suppose that the place of meeting of the lines by which the shadows are formed, prolonged backwards into the tube, is the place which is the seat of action of these rays? I think we have not. If a portion of the Crookes' tube which is influenced by the cathode discharge be isolated by, we will say, a lead screen containing a small hole, you get a portion of the cathodic rays which come out through that small hole, and you can trace what becomes of them beyond. It is found that the influence is decidedly stronger in a normal direction than in oblique directions. Professor

44

RÖNTGEN RAYS

J. J. Thomson, of Cambridge, who has worked a great deal experimentally at this subject, mentioned that to me as a striking thing. You might imagine that the fact that the shadows appear to be cast approximately from a source within the tube could be accounted for in this way. Supposing, as Röntgen believed, that the seat of the rays is in the place where the cathode discharge falls on the surface of the glass, those which come in an oblique direction have to pass through a greater thickness of glass than those which come in a normal direction. Now, glass is only partially transparent to the Röntgen rays; therefore the oblique rays would be more absorbed in passing through the glass than the rays which come in a normal direction. I mentioned that to Professor Thomson, but he said he thought the difference between the intensity of the rays which come out obliquely and those which come out in a normal direction was much too great to be accounted for in that way.* I will take it as a fact, without entering at present into any speculation as to the reason for it, that the Röntgen rays do come out from the glass wall more copiously in a normal direction than in an oblique direction. Assuming this, we can rightly say that

* I have found by subsequent inquiry that the experiment referred to was not made by Professor Thomson himself, but by Mr. C. M. McClelland, in the Cavendish Laboratory, and that on being recently repeated with the same tube the effect of the X-rays was found to be by no means so much concentrated towards the normal to the wall of the tube as in the former experiment. It seems likely that the difference may have been due to use of the tube in the interval, which would have made the exhaustion higher, and caused the X-rays given out to be of higher penetrative power, so as to render the increased thickness of glass which the rays emerging obliquely had to pass through to be of less consequence. But the subject is still under examination. In consequence of the result obtained in the second experiment, the statement in the text should be less absolute; but it may very well have happened that in the experiments of others the conditions may more nearly have agreed with those of the first experiment, causing what we may call the resultant activity of the X-rays to have had a direction leaning towards the normal drawn from the point casting the shadow to the wall of the tube.

the results obtained by Prince Galitzin and M. v. Karnojitzky, and similar results obtained by others, do not by any
means prove that the seat of the rays is within the tube.
Suppose, for example, that the tube were spherical, and a portion of this spherical surface were reached by the cathodic
rays; if the Röntgen rays which passed outside came wholly,
we will say, in a normal direction, produce the directions
backwards and you will get the centre of the tube. But we
have no right to say from that that there is anything particular
going on in the centre of the spherical tube. The result is
perfectly compatible with Röntgen's original assertion, which I
believe to be true, as to the seat of the rays.

Everything tends to show that these Röntgen rays are something which, like rays of light, are propagated in the ether.
What, then, is the nature of this process going on in the ether?
Some of the properties of the Röntgen rays are very surprising,
and very unlike what we are in the habit of considering with
regard to rays of light. One of the most striking things is the
facility with which they go through bodies which are utterly
opaque to light, such, for example, as black paper, board, and
so forth. If that stood alone it would, perhaps, not constitute
a very important difference between them and light. A red
glass will stop green rays and let red rays through; and just in
the same way if the Röntgen rays were of the nature of the ordinary rays of light, it is possible that a substance, although
opaque to light, might be transparent to them. So, as I say,
that remarkable property, if it stood alone, would not necessarily constitute any great difference of nature between them
and ordinary light. But there are other properties which are
far more difficult to reconcile with the idea that the Röntgen
rays are of the nature of light. There is the absence, or almost
complete absence, of refraction and reflection. Another remarkable property of these rays is the extreme sharpness of the
shadows which they cast when the source of the rays is made
sufficiently narrow. The shadows are far sharper than those
produced under similar circumstances by light, because in the
case of light the shadows are enlarged as the effect of diffrac-

tion. This absence, or almost complete absence, of diffraction is then another circumstance distinguishing these rays from ordinary rays of light. In face of these remarkable differences, those who speculated with regard to the nature of the rays were naturally disposed to look in a direction in which there was some distinct difference from the process which we conceive to go on in the propagation and production of ordinary rays of light. Those who have speculated on the dynamical theory of double refraction have been led to imagine the possible existence in the ether of longitudinal vibrations, as well as those transversal vibrations which we know to constitute light. If we were to suppose that the Röntgen rays are due to longitudinal vibrations, that would constitute such a very great difference of nature between them and rays of light that a very great difference in properties might reasonably be expected. But assuming that the Röntgen rays are a process which goes on in the ether, are the vibrations belonging to them normal or transversal ? If we could obtain evidence of the polarization of those rays, that would prove that the vibrations were not normal, but transversal. But if we fail to obtain evidence of polarization, that does not at once prove that the vibrations may not after all be transversal, because the properties of these rays are such as to lead us *à priori* to expect great difficulties in the way of putting in evidence their polarization, if, indeed, they are capable of polarization at all. Several experimentalists have attempted, by means of tourmalines, to obtain evidence of polarization, but the result in general has been negative. Of the two photographic markings that ought to be of unequal intensity on the supposition of polarization, one could not say with certainty that one was darker than the other. Another way of obtaining polarized light is by reflection at the proper angle from glass or other substance ; but, unfortunately for the success of such a method, the Röntgen rays refuse to be regularly reflected, except to a very small extent indeed. The authors of the paper to which I have already referred appear to have had some success with the tourmaline. Like others who have worked at the same experiment, they took a tourmaline cut parallel to the axis and put on top of it two others, also cut parallel to the axis, and of equal thickness, which were placed with their axes parallel and perpendicular respectively to that of the under tourmaline. But they supplemented this method by a device which is not explained in the paper itself, although a memoir is referred to in which the explanation is to be found —at least by those who can read the Russian language, which, unfortunately, I cannot. I can, therefore, only guess what the method was. It is something depending on the superposition of sensitive photographic films. I suspect they had several photographic films superposed, took the photographs on these, and then took them asunder for development, and after development put them together again as they had been originally. They consider that they have succeeded in obtaining evidence of a certain amount of polarization. If we assume that evidence to be undoubted, it decides the question at once. But as the experiment, as made in this way, is rather a delicate one, it is important for the evidence that we should consider as well what we may call the Becquerel rays. If time permits, I shall have something to say about these towards the close of my lecture, but, for the present, I shall say merely that they appear to be intermediate in their properties between the Röntgen rays and rays of ordinary light. The Becquerel rays undoubtedly admit of polarization, and the evidence appears on the whole pretty conclusive that the Röntgen rays, like rays of ordinary light, are due to transversal, and not to longitudinal, vibrations. It remains to be explained, if we can explain it, wherein lies the difference between the nature of the Röntgen rays and rays of ordinary light which accounts for the strange and remarkable difference in the properties of the two. I may mention that, although Cauchy and Neumann, and some others who have written on the dynamical theory of double refraction, have been led to the contemplation of normal vibrations, Green has put forward what seems to me a very strong argument against the existence of normal vibrations in the case of light. The argument Green used always weighed strongly with me against the supposition that the Röntgen rays were due to longitudinal vibrations; and the experiments by which, as I conceive, the possibility of their polarization has now been established go completely in the same direction, showing that they are due, assuming them to be some process going on in the ether, to a transversal disturbance of some kind.

Now, the so-called cathodic rays are, as we may say, the parents of the Röntgen rays. Consequently, if we are to explain the nature of the Röntgen rays, it is very important that we should have as clear ideas as may be permissible of the nature of the cathodic rays. Now, two views have been entertained as to the nature of the cathodic rays. According to one view, they are not rays of light at all, but streams of molecules which are projected from the cathode, and, if the exhaustion within the tube be sufficient, reach the opposite wall. That was the idea under which Crookes worked in his well-known experiments, and, so far as I know, it is the view held by all physicists in this country. Another opinion, however, has been published, and there are some eminent physicists who favor it, especially, I think, in Germany. According to this latter opinion, the cathodic rays are, like rays of light, some process going on in the ether. The cathodic ray, coming from the cathode towards the opposite wall of the tube, is invisible as such if you look across it. There is in reality a faint blue light ordinarily, but not necessarily, seen when you look across it. Lenard, in his most elaborate and remarkable experiments, succeeded in producing the cathodic rays within a space from which the gas was so very nearly completely taken away that, although the cathodic rays passed freely through the space, there was no appearance of the blue light when you viewed their path transversely. They produced, however, the ordinary effect of phosphorescence at the other end of the tube. The appearance, then, may be analogous to that of a sunbeam coming from a hole in the clouds. If it were not for the slight amount of dust and suspended matter in the air, the sunbeam would be invisible if you looked across it. But as the air is never free from motes, you see the path of the sunbeam when you look across it by the light reflected from these

D 49

motes. Something of the same kind may be conceived to take place with regard to the cathodic rays if they are some process going on in the ether. But there are very great difficulties in the way of this second hypothesis, and especially as regards certain properties of the cathodic rays. In the first place, they act mechanically. In Crookes' experiments he succeeded in causing a light windmill, if I may so describe it, to spin rapidly under the action of the rays. And when they were received on a very thin film of blown glass, the glass was actually bent under them as they fell upon it. But that is not all. These cathodic rays appear to proceed in a normal direction from the cathode, and ordinarily proceed in straight lines. But—and this is the important point—they are capable of being deflected in their path both by electro-static force and by magnetic or electro-dynamic force. Nothing whatever of the kind occurs with rays of light, and there are enormous, almost insuperable, difficulties in the supposition of any such deflection occurring if the cathodic rays are a process going on in the ether. I will not go into all the arguments for and against the two views, especially as the cathodic rays only enter incidentally into the subject I have chosen to bring before you. I will confine myself to one or two of the chief difficulties in the way of the supposition that the cathodic rays are streams of molecules. In his admirable experiments Lenard produced the cathodic rays in a tube which was highly exhausted, but not exhausted to the very highest degree that art can obtain. When you get to such tremendous exhaustions as that you cannot get the discharge to pass through the tube. What did he do? Previous experiments had shown that certain metals—aluminium especially—are, or appear to be, to a certain extent transparent to these rays. Working on the supposition that an aluminium plate is, to a certain extent, transparent to these rays, Lenard constructed a tube, highly exhausted, but not to the very last degree. Then a window of aluminium-foil—a very small aperture for mechanical reasons—was fastened in an air-tight manner at the end of the tube, to lead into a second tube provided with a phosphorescent screen. The cathodic rays produced in the first tube fell upon the aluminium plate and, as Lenard supposed, passed through it as rays of light would pass through glass. And so he got them into the second tube, and, it not being necessary to make an electric discharge pass through the second tube, he could exhaust it to the very highest power of skill that he had. It was a work of days and days. The cathodic rays behaved in this very highly exhausted tube like ordinary cathodic rays. We are asked to assume that we are dealing here with a vacuum, and according to Lenard that shows—and no doubt it would if we grant the assumption—that it is no longer a question of matter, but of some process going on in the ether.* And, apparently on the strength of that very elaborate experiment, Röntgen in his first paper seems to have been of the opinion that the cathodic rays were something going on in the ether. But are we justified in assuming that we are here dealing with a perfect vacuum? I do not think we are. I believe it passes the power of art to produce a perfect vacuum. You always have a little residue of which you cannot absolutely get rid, and some of Lenard's own figures show the effect of the residual gas. He isolated by screens a small part of the cathodic discharge in the second tube, and received it on a phosphorescent screen. He represents the phosphorescent light in the tube as consisting of a bright nucleus surrounded by a less bright halo. The bright nucleus was such as would be produced if the cathodic rays were rays of light, provided that that light were incapable of diffraction. But, then, how do you account for the halo? The blue light by which the cathodic rays are seen under ordinary circumstances is due, I believe, to an interference of the projected molecules with the molecules of the gas. In some of Lenard's experiments he received the cathodic rays in the first tube into the air, and a considerable amount of this blue light was seen. The appearance was much as if you had admitted a beam of light into a

* Even if the vacuum were perfect, and the result were still the same, that would not disprove the theory that the cathodic rays are streams of molecules, for the molecules might have been obtained from the aluminium window itself.

mixture of milk and water. To my mind this fainter halo in the most refined of Lenard's experiments, lying outside this well-defined nucleus, was evidence that the vacuum, in spite of all the skill and time expended upon it, was not perfect. And for aught we know to the contrary—I believe, indeed, it is the case—the cathodic rays in the second highly exhausted tube were really streams of molecules coming from the residual gas in the tube. But now comes a difficulty with regard to the passage of the cathodic rays through an aluminium plate. If the cathodic rays were something going on in the ether we might very well understand that an aluminium plate might be transparent to them although opaque to ordinary rays of light. But if the cathodic rays are really streams of molecules, how can we imagine that they get through the plate? Do they get through the plate? I do not believe they do. Do they riddle the plate like a bullet going through a thin piece of board? I do not think it. Suppose you have a trough containing a solution of sulphate of copper, and at the ends of it you have two copper plates; if you send an electric current through the trough, copper is eaten away at the anode and deposited at the cathode. Now, suppose you divide this trough into two by a plate of copper, you still have copper eaten away at the original anode and copper deposited at the original cathode. The interposed plate really divides the cell into two, in each of which electrolysis goes on, so that you have not only copper eaten away at one end of the trough and deposited at the other, but in your interposed plate you have copper eaten away at one side and deposited at the other. So it may be that the second surface of the aluminium-foil becomes, as it were, a new cathode, and starts cathodic rays. This, perhaps, is not what we should have anticipated beforehand. Still, there is nothing unnatural in it, and nothing, it seems to me, in consequence of which you would be obliged to reject the theory which makes the cathodic rays to be streams of molecules. There are one or two other difficulties mentioned by Wiedemann, but I do not think they are at all serious; they are certainly not so serious as the one I have just referred to. I will, therefore, pass on. The possibility of deflecting the cathodic rays by electrostatic and magnetic forces seems to be an insuperable difficulty in the way of the theory which makes them to be a process going on in the ether; but both of these are perfectly in accordance with what was to be expected on the supposition that they are streams of molecules, provided you remember that these molecules are highly charged with electricity. A moving charged body behaves as regards deflection like an electric current. Again, if you have highly charged molecules in the neighborhood of a positively or negatively statically charged body, they will be attracted or repelled, and the deflections of the rays are precisely what was to be expected according to that theory. I think we may assume that the cathodic rays are really streams of electrified molecules which strike against the opposite wall of the tube, or, as I will now call it, the target. Now, when a molecule, coming in this way from the cathode, strikes the target, how does the molecule act? It may act in two ways. It may act as a mass of matter, infinitesimal though it be, by virtue of its momentum —by virtue of its mass and velocity—and it may act also as a charged body, a statically charged body. What the appropriate physical idea is of a statically charged body is more than I can tell you. I was talking not long ago to Lord Kelvin about it—and he is a far higher authority in electrical matters than I am — and he considers that the physical idea of a statically charged body is still a mystery to us. Well, if these charged molecules strike the target we may think it exceedingly probable that by virtue of their charge they produce some sort of disturbance in the ether. This disturbance in the ether would spread in all directions from the place of disturbance, so that each projected molecule would on that supposition become, on reaching the target, a source of ethereal disturbance spreading in all directions. Well, what is the character of such a disturbance? The problem of diffraction, dynamically considered, may be supposed to reduce itself to this. Suppose you have an infinite mass of an elastic medium, and suppose a small portion is disturbed in the most general way possible, what will take place ? A wave of disturbance will spread out spherically from the place of disturbance.* You might at first sight suppose that you could have a wave, in any limited region of which you might have a transversal disturbance in some one direction, the same all through the thickness of the shell occupied by the wave, though naturally the direction of disturbance might vary from one region to another more or less distant region. But the dynamical theory shows that that is not possible. In any limited region, or elementary area, as we may regard it, of the wave, as you pass in a direction perpendicular to the front, the disturbance in one direction must be exchanged for a disturbance in the opposite direction, in such a manner that ultimately—that is, when the radius of the wave is very large compared with its thickness—the integral of the disturbance in one direction, which we may designate as positive, must be balanced by the integral of the disturbance in the opposite, or negative, direction. The simplest sort of "pulse," as I will call it, in order to distinguish it from a periodic undulation, would be one consisting of two halves in which the disturbances were in opposite directions. The positive and negative parts are not necessarily alike, as one may make up by a greater width, measured in the direction of propagation, for a smaller amplitude ; but it will be simplest to think of them as alike, except as to sign. The following figure represents this conception, the positive and negative halves being distinguished by a difference of shading.

According to the view here put forward, the Röntgen emanation consists of a vast succession of independent pulses, starting respectively from the points and at the times at which the individual charged molecules projected from the cathode impinge on the target. At first sight it might appear as if mere pulses would be inadequate to account for

* If the medium be compressible there will be two waves, that which travels the more swiftly consisting of normal vibrations ; but the opinion has already been expressed that it is transversal vibrations with which we are concerned.

the effects produced, seeing that in the case of light we have to deal with series consisting each of a very great number of consecutive undulations. But we must bear in mind how vast, according to our theoretical views, must be the number of molecules contained in the smallest quantity of ponderable matter of which we can take cognizance by our senses. Hence, small as is the quantity of matter projected in a given short time from the cathode, it may yet be sufficient to give rise to pulses the number of which is inconceivably great. It remains to consider in what way this conception may enable us to explain the most striking properties of the Röntgen rays in relation to the contrasts which they offer to rays of light.

The most elementary difference, as being one which has relation only to propagation in the ether, consists in the absence, or, at any rate, almost complete absence, of diffraction. As the different pulses are by hypothesis quite independent of one another, we have to explain this phenomenon for a single pulse.

In the figure let CB be a portion of a spherical pulse spreading outwards from the centre of disturbance (which I will call O) from which it came, P a point in front of the wave, where the disturbance which will arrive there is sought. From P let fall a normal PQ on the front of the wave, and let AB, taken around Q, be a small portion of the spherical shell which at the present 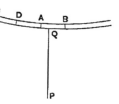 moment is the seat of the pulse, and suppose the breadth of AB to be small compared with PQ and with the radius of the shell, but large compared with the shell's thickness. Let CD be an element of the shell of similar size to AB, but situated in a direction from P distinctly inclined to PQ; and supposing all the disturbance in the shell stopped except what occupies one or other of the elements AB, CD, let us inquire what will be the disturbance subsequently produced at P in the two cases respectively.

55

I have shown elsewhere* that in our present problem the disturbance at P is expressed by a double integral taken over such portion of the surface of a sphere with P for centre and bt for radius (b being the velocity of propagation) as lies within the disturbed region, which in this case is the spherical shell or a part of it. It will be convenient to think of a series of spheres drawn round P with radii bt for increasing values of t. When t is such that the sphere just touches the shell at Q, and then goes on increasing, the disturbance is nearly the same all over that portion of the surface of the sphere which lies within the small region AB, and that, whether we take the portion of the expression for the disturbance at P which depends on the disturbance (displacement or velocity) at the surface of the sphere whose radius is bt, or the portion which depends on the differential coefficient of the displacement or velocity with respect to a radius vector drawn from O. Consequently the positive and negative parts of the disturbance will reach P in succession. But if instead of the small portion AB of the shell we take CD, lying in a direction from P not very near the normal, it is easy to see that the positive and negative parts of the disturbance expressed by our double integral, reaching as they do P simultaneously, almost completely cancel each other. And this cancelling is so much more nearly complete as the obliquity is greater, and likewise as the thickness of the shell is smaller. If, then, the disturbance in the ether consequent on the arrival of any projected molecule at the target is very prompt, lasting, it may be, only a very small fraction of the period of a single vibration of the ether in the case of light, our shell will be so thin that a small isolated portion of the Röntgen discharge is propagated so nearly wholly in the direction of a normal to the wave that the almost complete absence of diffraction is thus accounted for.†

* "On the Dynamical Theory of Diffraction," *Cambridge Philosophical Transactions*, vol. ix., p. 1; or *Collected Papers*, vol. ii., p. 243, Arts. 19–22.

† It is known that there is a difference of quality in Röntgen rays, and that the Röntgen discharge may be filtered by absorption. It is known also that the increased exhaustion in a Crookes' tube, which is accompanied

The explanation which has just been given of the apparent absence of diffraction in the case of the Röntgen rays is closely analogous to the ordinary explanation of the existence of rays and shadows. It differs, however, in this respect, that here we are dealing with a single pulse, whereas in the case of light we are dealing with an indefinite succession of disturbances. In order to understand the sharpness of the shadows produced by the Röntgen rays, we are not obliged to suppose that the disturbance is periodic at all. It must be partly negative and partly positive, and that being the case, if the thickness of the shell is very small, the amount of diffraction will be very small, too. Those who have attempted to obtain evidence of the diffraction of the Röntgen rays have been led to the conclusion that if the rays are periodic at all the period is something enormously small—perhaps thirty times, perhaps a hundred times, as small as the wave-length of green light. It seems difficult to imagine by what process you could get such very small vibrations, if vibrations there be. It is easier to understand how the arrival of charged molecules at the cathode might produce disturbances which are almost abrupt.

Well, then, this is what I conceive to constitute the Röntgen rays. You have a rain of molecules coming from the electrically charged cathode, which you may think of as the rain-drops in a shower. They strike successively on the target, each molecule on striking the target producing a pulse, as I have called it, in the ether, which is essentially partly positive and partly negative; and you have a vast succession of these pulses coming from the various points of the target which are not protected by some screen interposed for the purpose of experiment.

by increasing difficulty in sending a discharge through it, has the effect of giving rise to increasing penetrative power in the Röntgen rays which it gives out. It seems to me probable that this difference of quality corresponds to a more or less close approach to perfect abruptness in the production of disturbance in the ether when a molecule propelled from the cathode reaches the target, and accordingly to a less or a greater thickness in the outward-travelling shell of disturbance in the ether; and that at relatively high exhaustions the molecules are propelled with a higher velocity, and so give rise to a more prompt disturbance when they reach the target.

This explains the absence, or almost complete absence, of diffraction. But that is not all we have to explain; we have still a very serious thing behind. What is it that constitutes the difference between the Röntgen rays and rays of ordinary light in consequence of which the one are not refracted, or only in an infinitesimal degree, while the other are freely refracted? This difficulty led me to conceive of a theory, which I believe to be new, as to the nature of refraction itself—as to the nature of what takes place, for example, when light is refracted through a prism. Suppose we have light of a definite refrangibility, and a prism on which it may be made to fall. When the light is admitted we commonly imagine—at least, I believe so—that the light is immediately refracted, and with proper appliances you get the spectrum. Immediately? I do not think so. How is it that light travels more slowly through refracting medium than through vacuum? There are different conjectures which have been advanced. One is that the ether within refracting media is more dense than the ether in free space. Another is that while the density is the same the elasticity is less. Then, there have been speculations as to the ether being loaded with particles of matter.

Take a piano. If you strike a note a string is set in vibration. You would hardly hear any sound at all if it were rigidly supported. But it rests on a bridge communicating with a sounding-board, and the sounding-board presents a broad surface to the air, and is set in motion by the string. The sounding-board and the string form a compound vibrating system. In the same way it may be that the molecules of the glass, or other refracting medium, and the ether form between them a compound vibrating system, and, *when the motion is fully established*, the two vibrate harmoniously together. But how does it get to be established? We can hardly imagine otherwise than that the ether is excessively rare compared with ponderable matter.* Well, supposing the ethereal vibrations start and

* The views as to the nature of refraction, which I have endeavored to explain, lead me incidentally to make a remark on another subject not, indeed, very closely connected with it. From the first, Röntgen recognized as

reach a set of molecules, they are somewhat impeded by the molecules, and they tend also to move the molecules. But as the molecules are relatively very heavy, it may be that it takes

the seat of the X-rays which he had discovered the place where the cathodic rays fall on the wall of the Crookes' tube. This place is indicated to the eye by the fluorescence of the glass. But we are not on that account to regard the fluorescence as the cause of the Röntgen rays, or even to regard the Röntgen emission as a sort of fluorescence. I have seen it remarked, as indicating no very close connection between the two, that with a metallic target we have a copious emission of Röntgen rays though there is no fluorescence, and that when a spot on the glass wall of a Crookes' tube has for some time been exposed to a rather concentrated cathodic discharge, though the fluorescence which it exhibits under the action of the cathodic discharge becomes comparatively dull, as if the glass were in some way fatigued for fluorescence, it emits the Röntgen rays as well as before.

Fluorescence is undoubtedly indicative of a molecular disturbance ; but in what precise way this disturbance is brought about by the cathodic discharge is a matter on which I refrain from speculating. But whatever be the precise nature of the process, it seems pretty evident that it can only be by repeated impacts of molecules from the cathode that a sufficient molecular disturbance can be got up to show itself as a visible fluorescence.

Suppose a shower of molecules from the cathode to be allowed suddenly to fall on the anti-cathode, and after raining on it for a little to be as suddenly cut off. According to the views I entertain as to the nature of the Röntgen rays, the moment the shower is let on the emission of Röntgen rays begins, it lasts as long as the shower, and ceases the moment the shower is cut off. But the fluorescence only gradually, quickly though it may be, comes on when the shower is allowed to fall, and gradually fades away when the shower is cut off. So far from the fluorescence being in any way the cause of the Röntgen emission, there seems reason to think that if it exercises any effect upon it at all, it is rather adverse than favorable. For it has been found that when the target is metallic, and gets heated, the Röntgen discharge falls off ; and fluorescence, like a rise of temperature, involves a molecular disturbance, though the kind of disturbance is different in the two cases.

As the fluorescence of the glass wall and the emission of X-rays are two totally different effects of the same cause — namely, the molecular bombardment from the cathode—the intensity of the one must by no means be taken as a measure of the intensity of the other, even with the same tube. The former effect would appear to be the more easily produced. This consideration removes a difficulty mentioned at page 10 of the paper some considerable time for the molecules to be set sensibly in motion. Now if the system of molecules is exceedingly complex, a mode of motion of the molecules, or it may be of the constituent parts of the molecules, may be found such that the system tends to vibrate in practically any periodic time that you may choose; only as you choose one time or another the mode of vibration will be different; and, again, according to the direction in which the molecules are successively made to vibrate the actual mode of vibration will be different. Well, I conceive that the difference between the propagation of the Röntgen rays and rays of ordinary light with reference to passing through a prism depends upon that. When you let a ray of light fall upon a refracting medium such as glass, motions begin to take place in the molecules forming the medium. The motion is at first more or less irregular; but the vibrations ultimately settle down into a system of such a kind that the regular joint vibrations of the molecules and of the ether are such as correspond to a given periodic time, namely, that of the light before incidence on the medium. That particular kind of vibration among the molecules is kept up, while the others die away, so that after a prolonged time—the time occupied by, we will say, ten thousand vibrations, which is only about the forty-thousand-millionth part of a second—the motion of the molecules of the glass has gradually got up until you have the molecules of the glass and the ether vibrating harmoniously together. But in the case of the Röntgen rays, if the nature of them be what I have explained, you have a constant succession of pulses independent of one another. Consequently there is no chance to get up harmony between the vibrations of the ether and the vibrations of the body.

Go back to the case of light passing through glass. When

by Prince Galitzin and M. v. Karnojitzky, as attending the supposition that the X-rays originate in the points in which the cathodic rays fall on the wall of the tube or other target. Nor need it surprise us that in some cases the shadows seem to indicate more than one source of action, when we remember that from a given point more than one normal can be drawn to a given closed surface.

the regular combined vibration is established you have a kinetic energy, due partly to the motion of the ether and partly to the motion of the molecules. If you make abstraction of the loss of energy by reflection, the rate at which the energy passes within the glass must be the same as it has outside, and consequently there must be the same energy for one wave length, which corresponds to one period of the vibration, inside as outside. But if the kinetic energy of the ether is the same for the same volume inside and outside, and you have in addition inside a certain amount of kinetic energy due to the motion of the molecules, the two taken together can only make the energy for a wave inside the same as for a wave outside on the condition that the velocity of propagation inside is less than the velocity of propagation outside. That is the theory I have been forced to adopt as to the nature of refraction in consequence of the ideas I hold as to the nature of the Röntgen rays ; and if you adopt that theory I think everything falls into its place. When you have the Röntgen rays falling on a body, the motion of the ether due to them is interfered with by the molecules of the body, more or less. No body is perfectly transparent to these rays, and, on the other hand, perhaps we may say no body is perfectly opaque. That all falls into its place on this supposition as to the nature of the action of the ether on the molecules. Now, why is it that the Röntgen rays do not care whether you present them with black paper or white paper ? What is the cause of blackness ? The light falling upon the paper produces motion in the ultimate molecules. In the case of a transparent substance you have a compound vibrating system going on, vibrating without change. But in the case of an absorbing medium the vibrations which after a time are produced in the molecules spread out into adjoining molecules, by virtue of the communication of the molecules with one another, and are carried away ; so that in the case of an absorbing medium there is a constant beginning to set the molecules in vibration ; but they never get to the permanent state, because the vibration is carried away by communication from one molecule to another. But in the case of

61

the Röntgen rays you have done with the pulse altogether
long before any harmonious vibration between the ether and
the molecules can be established ; so that a state of things is
not brought about in which you get a, comparatively speaking,
large vibration of the molecules. Consequently, the Röntgen
rays do not care whether you give them black paper or not.

I must not keep you more than a minute or two longer ; but
I do not like to close this lecture without saying a word or
two regarding the Becquerel rays. What takes place there ?
To be brief, I must refer to the most striking case of all.
Take the case of metallic uranium. That gives out something
which, like the Röntgen rays, has an influence passing through
black paper, and capable of affecting a photographic plate.
It is also capable of effecting the discharge of statically charged
electrified bodies. Apparently this goes on indefinitely. You
do not need, apparently, to expose the metal to rays of high
refrangibility in order that this strange thing should go on.
What takes place ? My conjecture is that the molecule of
uranium has a structure which may be roughly compared to a
flexible chain with a small weight at the end of it. Suppose
you have vibrations communicated to such a chain at the top ;
they travel gradually to the bottom, and near the bottom produce a disturbance which deviates more from a simple har-
monic undulation. So, if a vibration is communicated to
what I will call the tail of the molecule of uranium, it may
give rise to a disturbance in the ether which is not of a regular
periodic character. I conceive, then, that you have vibrations
produced in the ether, not of such a permanently regular character as would constitute them vibrations of light, and yet not
of so simple a character as in the Röntgen rays—something between. And accordingly there is enough irregularity to allow
the ethereal disturbance to pass through black paper, and
enough regularity on the other hand to make possible a certain amount of refraction. You can also obtain evidence of
the polarization, and, consequently, of the transverse character
of these rays.

According to the theory of the nature of the Röntgen rays

which I have endeavored very briefly to bring before you, we have here, as I think, a system the various parts of which fit into one another. You start with the Röntgen rays, which consist, as I conceive, of an enormous succession of independent pulses; you pass to the Becquerel rays, which are still irregular, but are beginning to have a certain amount of regularity; and you end with the rays which constitute ordinary light. According to this theory, the absence of diffraction in the Röntgen rays is explained, not by supposing they are rays of light of excessively short wave length, but by supposing they are due to an irregular repetition of isolated and independent disturbances. So far as I know, the view I have been led to form as to the nature of refraction, and which forms an integral portion of the theory as to the Röntgen rays, is altogether new, so much so that I felt at first rather startled by it; but I found myself fairly driven to it by the ideas I entertain as to the nature of the Röntgen rays, and I am not aware of any serious objection to it.

ADDITIONAL NOTE

The problem of diffraction in the case of a vast system of *independent* very slender pulses deserves to be treated in somewhat greater detail. It is rather simpler than the problem of diffraction in the case of series of undulations such as those which constitute light, because the pulses are to be treated separately and independently, like streams of light from different sources; and as the whole thickness of a pulse in the case of the Röntgen rays may probably be something comparable with the millionth of an inch, we have no need to inquire what will be the disturbance continually passing across a fixed surface in space; we may treat the shell at any moment as constituting an initial disturbance in the ether, and then examine the efficiency of different parts of the shell in disturbing at a future time the ether at a given point of space in front of the shell.

The thickness of the shell is not necessarily the same at points situated in widely different directions as regards their bearing from the centre, and the same applies to the direction

63

of disturbance. But in any case for a small portion of the shell the thickness may be deemed uniform, and the direction of disturbance sensibly the same as we pass from point to point in a direction tangential to the shell, while it varies with great rapidity, at least as regards its amount, when we pass from point to point in a normal direction, vanishing at the outer and inner boundaries of the shell.

As the disturbance we are concerned with is of the distor-

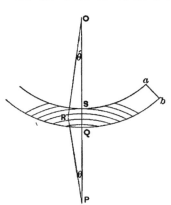

tional kind only, the disturbance at time t at a point P in front of the shell may be obtained from that at time 0 in the shell in its position which is taken as initial by the last equation in Art. 22 of my paper on diffraction already cited. Let R be a point in the shell of disturbance when in that position which is regarded as initial, r, r' the distances PR, OR; θ, θ' their inclinations to OP; ϕ the azimuth round OP of the plane PRO. Then in the formula referred to $d\sigma = \sin\theta\, d\theta\, d\phi$. Also $rd\theta \times \sin(\theta+\theta') = dr'$; and $\sin\theta/\sin(\theta+\theta') = r'/OP = r'/(r+r')$ very nearly.

Let OP cut the inner boundary of the shell in S, and let ab or QS, the thickness of the shell, be denoted by λ. In the equation referred to, the term arising from the differentiation with respect to t of the t outside the sign of double integration will be of the order λ/r' as compared with the others, and may, therefore, be neglected. The t outside may be replaced by r/b, and the fraction $r/(r+r')$, being sensibly constant over the range of integration, may be put outside. Our expression then becomes

$$4\pi b\xi = \frac{r'}{r+r'}\int\int\left(u_0 - b\frac{d\xi_0}{dr'}\right)_{bt}dr'\,d\phi.\,*$$

* The suffix bt means that the integration is taken over a spherical surface with centre P and radius bt.

As the disturbance deemed initial was only a momentary condition of a wave that had been travelling outwards with the velocity b, we must have $u_0 = -b\dfrac{d\xi_0}{dr'}$, and therefore

$$2\pi\xi = -\frac{r'}{r+r'} \int \int \left(\frac{d\xi_0}{dr'}\right)_{bt} dr' d\phi.$$

The expression is left in the first instance in this shape in order to show more clearly the manner in which each portion of the disturbance in the state taken as initial contributes towards the future disturbance at P. When there is no obstacle to the transmission we shall have $\int d\phi = 2\pi$, and $\int \left(\dfrac{d\xi_0}{dr'}\right)_{bt} dr' = (\xi_0)_{bt}$ taken between limits. If $bt < PQ$, the sphere round P with radius bt does not cut the disturbed region at all, and the disturbance at P is nil. If $bt > PS$, the limits of r' are the distances from O at which the sphere round P cuts the inner and outer limits of the shell, and as the disturbance there vanishes we have again no disturbance at P. But if bt lies between those limits, and the sphere round P cuts OP in T (which point must lie between Q and S) the limits of r' will be OT to a point in the outer boundary of the shell, where therefore ξ_0 vanishes. Hence the displacement at P is the same as was initially at T, only diminished in the ratio of $r+r'$ to r', as we know it ought to be.

Reverting to the expression for ξ given by the double integral, we see that the only portion of the shell which is efficient in producing a subsequent disturbance at P lies between the sphere round O with radius OQ and the sphere round P with radius PS. If β be the distance from OP of the intersection of these spheres, we have, considering the smallness of the obliquities,

$$\beta^2 = \frac{2rr'\lambda}{r+r'}.$$

If we suppose r and r' to be each 4 inches, and λ the millionth of an inch, we have $\beta = 0.002$ inch, so that at a distance not less than the one-250th of an inch from the projection of the edge of an opaque body intercepting Röntgen rays coming from a point 4 inches off, and received on a screen (fluorescent or photographic) 4 inches on the other side, there would be full effect or no effect according as we take the illuminated or the dark side of the projection. We see then how possible it may be to have an almost complete absence of diffraction of the Röntgen rays if the pulses are as thin as above supposed ; and as these rays are started in the first instance in a totally different manner from rays of ordinary light, namely, by the arrival of charged molecules from a cathode at a target instead of by the vibrations of the molecules of ponderable matter, we know of no reason beforehand forbidding us to attribute an excessive thinness to the pulses which the charged molecules excite in the ether.

***

BIOGRAPHICAL SKETCH

SIR GEORGE GABRIEL STOKES was born August 13, 1819, in Ireland, County Sligo, and is at the present time Fellow of Pembroke College and Lucasian Professor of Mathematics in the University of Cambridge. He was Senior Wrangler in 1841 ; he has been President of the Royal Society of London, and has received numerous honors at home and abroad. His main contributions to science may be grouped under the head of Hydrodynamics and the Wave Theory of Light. His papers on the former subject gave the first rigid treatment and formed the basis of our modern theory. Similarly, in the wave theory of light his papers on the dynamical theory of diffraction and on the aberration of light are two of the most important contributions of modern times to science. His collected papers are being published at the present time by the University of Cambridge, and two volumes have already appeared.

His experimental work has been largely in connection with such optical phenomena as fluorescence, metallic reflection, and certain anomalous colors seen in crystals.

His mathematical work is of the first importance, and his numerous contributions to all branches of mathematical physics have been of the greatest service to science.

A THEORY OF THE CONNECTION BE-TWEEN CATHODE AND RÖNTGEN RAYS

BY

J. J. THOMSON, M.A., F.R.S.,

Cavendish Professor of Experimental Physics, Cambridge

(*Philosophical Magazine*, February, 1898)

CONTENTS

A THEORY OF THE CONNECTION BE-TWEEN CATHODE AND RÖNTGEN RAYS

BY

J. J. THOMSON, M.A., F.R.S.

A moving electrified particle is surrounded by a magnetic field, the lines of magnetic force being circles having the line of motion of the particle for axis. If the particle be suddenly stopped, there will, in consequence of electro-magnetic induction, be no instantaneous change in the magnetic field; the induction gives rise to a magnetic field which for a moment compensates for that destroyed by the stopping of the particle. The new field thus introduced is not, however, in equilibrium, but moves off through the dielectric as an electric pulse. In this paper we calculate the magnetic force and electric intensity carried by the pulse to any point in the dielectric.

The distribution of magnetic force and electric intensity around the moving particle depends greatly on the velocity of the particle; if this velocity is so small that the square of its ratio to the velocity of light can be neglected, then the electric intensity is symmetrically distributed round the particle, and at a distance r from it is equal to e/r^2, where e is the charge on the particle; the lines of magnetic force are circles with the line of motion of the particle for axis; the magnitude of the magnetic force at a point P is $we \sin \theta / r^2$, where w is the velocity of the particle, and θ the angle a radius from the particle to P makes with the direction of motion.

When, however, the velocity of the particle is so great that

69

we can no longer neglect the square of its ratio to the velocity of light, the distribution of electric intensity is no longer uniform ; the electric intensity, along with the magnetic force, tends to concentrate in the equatorial plane—that is, the plane through the centre of the particle at right angles to its direction of motion ; this tendency increases with the velocity of the particle until, when this is equal to the velocity of light, both the magnetic force and the electric intensity vanish at all parts of the field, except the equatorial plane, and in this plane they are infinite.

The pulses started by the stopping of the charged particle are, as might be expected, different when the ratio of the velocity of the particle to that of light is small and when it is nearly unity. But even when the velocity is small, the pulse, started by stopping the particle, carries to an external point a disturbance in which the magnetic force is enormously greater than it was at the same point before the particle was stopped. The time the pulse takes to pass over a point P is, if the charged particle be spherical, equal to the time light takes to pass over a distance equal to the diameter of this sphere ; the thickness of this pulse is excessively small compared with the wave-length of visible light. When the velocity of the particle approaches. that of light, two pulses are started when it is stopped. One of these is a thin plane sheet whose thickness is equal to the diameter of the charged particle ; this wave is propagated in the direction in which the particle was moving ; there is no corresponding wave propagated backwards: the other is a spherical pulse, spreading outward in all directions, whose thickness is again equal to the diameter of the charged particle, and thus, if the particle is of molecular dimensions, or, perhaps, even smaller, very small compared with the wave-length of ordinary light. The theory I wish to put forward is that the Röntgen rays are these thin pulses of electric and magnetic disturbances which are started when the small negatively charged particles which constitute the cathode rays are stopped.

[*The mathematical theory is omitted.*]

Thus we see that the stoppage of a charged particle will give rise to very thin pulses of intense magnetic force and electric intensity; when the velocity of the particle is small there will be one spherical pulse; when the velocity is nearly equal to that of light there will, in addition to the spherical pulse, be a plane one, propagated only in the direction in which the particle was originally moving. It is these pulses which I believe constitute the Röntgen rays. As they consist of electric and magnetic disturbances, they might be expected to produce some effects analogous to those of light. If they were so thin that the time taken by them to pass over a molecule of a substance were small compared with the time of vibration of the molecule, there would be no refraction, and the thinness of the pulse would also account for the absence of diffraction.

In the preceding investigation we have supposed that the stoppage of the particle is instantaneous; if the impact lasts for a finite time T, the negative pulse will be broadened out, so that its thickness, instead of being $2a$, will be $2a + VT$, where V is the velocity of light. The intensity of the magnetic force in the pulse will vary inversely as the thickness of the pulse, so that, when the collision lasts for the time T, the magnetic force in the negative pulse will be $2a/(2a + VT)$ of the value given above. The more sudden the collision, the thinner the pulse and the greater the magnetic force and the energy in the pulse; the pulse will, however, possess the properties of the Röntgen rays until T is comparable to one of the times of vibration of a substance through which it has to pass. In the case of the cathode rays all the circumstances seem favorable to a very sudden collision, as the mass of the moving particles is very small and their velocity exceedingly great. In some experiments which I described in the *Philosophical Magazine* for October, 1897, on cathode rays, the velocity of the negative particles was about one-third of that of light, and in some more recent experiments made on the Lenard rays, with the apparatus described by Des Coudres, considerably higher velocities were found. A change in the time of the collision will alter the thickness of the pulse, and so change the nature of the ray.

If we suppose that part of the absorption of the rays is due to the communication of energy to charged ions in their path, we find that the thicker the pulse the greater the absorption. For, suppose that E is the electric intensity in the pulse, m the mass, and e the charge on an ion; then, if u is the velocity communicated to the ion when the pulse passes over it, t the time taken by the pulse to pass over it,

$$mu = Ee \cdot t ;$$

or, if d is the thickness of the pulse,

$$mu = Ee \cdot \frac{d}{V} ;$$

thus the energy $\frac{1}{2}mu^2$ communicated to the ion is equal to

$$\frac{1}{2} \frac{E^2 d^2 e^2}{V^2} .$$

Now the energy in the pulse is proportional to $E^2 d/V^2$, so that the ratio of the energy communicated to the ion to the energy in the pulse is proportional to d. Thus, the broader the pulse, the greater the absorption and the less the penetrating power. The energy in the pulse is inversely proportional to its thickness.

If we return to the expression for the intensity of the magnetic force in case (1), we see that it is proportional to $\sin \theta$, so that the disturbance is greatest at right angles to the cathode rays : thus, if the cathode particles are stopped at their first encounter, the Röntgen rays would be brightest at right angles to the cathode rays ; if, however, as would seem most probable, the cathode particles had to make several encounters before they were reduced to rest, changing their direction between each encounter, the distribution of the cathode rays would be much more uniform. Experiments on the distribution of Röntgen rays produced by the impact of the cathode particles directly against the walls of the discharge-tube are, as Sir George Stokes has pointed out, affected by the much greater absorption of the oblique rays produced by the greater thickness of glass traversed by them. Experiments on rays produced by focus-tubes would give results more easily interpreted.

RÖNTGEN RAYS

The result to which we have been led from the consideration
of the effects produced by the sudden stoppage of an electrified
particle, *viz.*, that the Röntgen effects are produced by a very
thin pulse of intense electro-magnetic disturbance, is in agreement with the view expressed by Sir George Stokes in the
Wilde Lecture ("Proceedings of the Manchester Literary and
Philosophical Society," 1897), that the Röntgen rays are not
waves of very short wave-length, but impulses.

Cambridge, *December* 16, 1897.

BIOGRAPHICAL SKETCH

JOSEPH JOHN THOMSON was born Dec. 18, 1856, in Manchester, and is at the present time Fellow of Trinity College and
the Cavendish Professor of Experimental Physics at Cambridge.
Professor Thomson was second Wrangler in 1880, and was appointed to his professorship in 1884. He has contributed
greatly to our knowledge of both practical and theoretical
physics; his researches on the theory of vortices, and on the
application of dynamics to physical problems, have been published in book form. The greatest debt that science owes
him, however, is for having introduced system and order into
the vast collection of experimental data which have been ac-
cumulated concerning the discharge of electricity through
gases. His work on this subject has been carried on during
the past ten years, and the most important conclusions are contained in his volume *Recent Researches in Electricity and Mag-
netism*, Oxford, 1893. Professor Thomson has contributed
largely to our present knowledge of cathode rays and to all
that pertains to the connection between matter and electricity,
particularly to the explanation of electrolysis and ionization.

73

BIBLIOGRAPHY

AMONG the most important papers bearing upon the subject of X-rays are the following :

CATHODE RAYS :

    Lenard, Wiedemann, *Annalen*, **51**, 1894 ; **56**, 1895 ; **63**, 1897.

    Thomson, J. J., *Philosophical Magazine*, **38**, 1894 ; **44**, 1897.
                    British Association Report, 1896.

    McClelland, *Proceedings Royal Society of London*, **61**, 1897.

    Perrin, *Comptes Rendus*, **121**, 1895.

RÖNTGEN RAYS :

    Thomson, J. J., *Proceedings Royal Society of London*, **59**, 1896.
               Nature, **53**, **54**, **55**, **58**, 1896–1898.

    Perrin, *Annales de Chimie et de Physique*, **11**, 1897.
          Comptes Rendus, **122**, **123**, **124**, **126**, 1896–1898.

    Murray, J. R. E., *Proceedings Royal Society of London*, **59**, 1896.

    Wilson, C. T. R., *Proceedings Royal Society of London*, **59**, 1896.

    Lehmann, *Zeitschrift für Electrochemie*, **1**, 1896.

    Lord Rayleigh, *Nature*, **57**, 1898.

    Les Rayons X et la Photographie à Travers les Corps Opaques. Par Ch.
        Ed. Guillaume, Paris, 1896.

    Röntgen Rays and Phenomena of the Anode and Cathode. By E. P.
        Thompson, New York, 1896.

BECQUEREL RAYS :

    Becquerel, H., *Comptes Rendus*, **122**, **123**, **124**, 1896–1897.

    Sagnac, G., *Journal de Physique*, **5**, 1896.

    *A Résumé of the Experiments dealing with the Properties of Becquerel
        Rays.* By O. M. Stewart, *Physical Review*, **6**, April, 1898.

THORIUM RAYS :

    Schmidt, G. C., Wiedemann, *Annalen*, **65**, 1898.

    Sklodowska-Curie, *Comptes Rendus*, **126**, 1898.

INDEX

INDEX

THE END

STANDARDS IN NATURAL SCIENCE

COMPARATIVE ZOOLOGY

Structural and Systematic. For use in Schools and Colleges. By JAMES ORTON, Ph.D. New edition, revised by CHARLES WRIGHT DODGE, M.S., Professor of Biology in the University of Rochester. With 350 illustrations. Crown 8vo, Cloth, $1 80; by mail, $1 96.

The distinctive character of this work consists in the treatment of the whole Animal Kingdom as a unit; in the comparative study of the development and variations of organs and their functions, from the simplest to the most complex state; in withholding Systematic Zoology until the student has mastered those structural affinities upon which true classification is founded; and in being fitted for High Schools and Mixed Schools by its language and illustrations, yet going far enough to constitute a complete grammar of the science for the undergraduate course of any college.

INTRODUCTION TO ELEMENTARY PRACTICAL BIOLOGY

A Laboratory Guide for High Schools and College Students. By CHARLES WRIGHT DODGE, M.S., Professor of Biology, University of Rochester. Crown 8vo, Cloth, $1 80; by mail, $1 95.

Professor Dodge's manual consists essentially of questions on the structure and the physiology of a series of common animals and plants typical of their kind—questions which can be answered only by actual examination of the specimen or by experiment. Directions are given for the collection of specimens, for their preservation, and for preparing them for examination; also for performing simple physiological experiments. Particular species are not required, as the questions usually apply well to several related forms.

THE STUDENTS' LYELL

A Manual of Elementary Geology. Edited by JOHN W. JUDD, C.B., LL.D., F.R.S., Professor of Geology, and Dean of the Royal College of Science, London. With a Geological Map, and 736 Illustrations in the Text. New, revised edition. Crown 8vo, Cloth, $2 25; by mail, $2 39.

The progress of geological science during the last quarter of a century has rendered necessary very considerable additions and corrections, and the rewriting of large portions of the book, but I have everywhere striven to preserve the author's plan and to follow the methods which characterize the original work.—*Extract from the Preface of the Revised Edition.*

NEW YORK AND LONDON
HARPER & BROTHERS, PUBLISHERS

TEXT-BOOKS IN PHYSICS

THEORY OF PHYSICS

By Joseph S. Ames, Ph.D., Associate Professor of Physics in
Johns Hopkins University.   Crown 8vo, Cloth, $1 60 ;
by mail, $1 75.

In writing this book it has been the author's aim to give a concise
statement of the experimental facts on which the science of physics is
based, and to present with these statements the accepted theories which
correlate or "explain" them. The book is designed for those students who
have had no previous training in physics, or at least only an elementary
course, and is adapted to junior classes in colleges or technical schools.
The entire subject, as presented in the work, may be easily studied in a
course lasting for the academic year of nine months.

Perhaps the best general introduction to physics ever printed in the
English language. . . . A model of comprehensiveness, directness, arrangement, and clearness of expression. . . . The treatment of each subject is
wonderfully up to date for a text-book, and does credit to the system
which keeps Johns Hopkins abreast of the times. Merely as an example
of lucid expression and of systematization the book is worthy of careful
reading.—*N. Y. Press.*

Seems to me to be thoroughly scientific in its treatment and to give
the student what is conspicuously absent in certain well-known text-books
on the subject—an excellent perspective of the very extensive phenomena
of physics. — Professor F. E. Beach, *Sheffield Scientific School of Yale
University.*

A MANUAL OF EXPERIMENTS IN PHYSICS

Laboratory Instruction for College Classes. By Joseph S.
Ames, Ph.D., Associate Professor of Physics in Johns
Hopkins University, author of "Theory of Physics," and
William J. A. Bliss, Associate in Physics in Johns Hop-
kins University. 8vo, Cloth, $1 80 ; by mail, $1 95.

I have examined the book, and am greatly pleased with it. It is clear
and well arranged, and has the best and newest methods. I can cheerfully
recommend it as a most excellent work of its kind.—H. W. Harding,
Professor Emeritus of Physics, Lehigh University.

I think the work will materially aid laboratory instructors, lead to
more scientific training of the students, and assist markedly in incentives
to more advanced and original research.—Lucien I. Blake, *Professor of
Physics, University of Kansas.*

It is written with that clearness and precision which are characteristic
of its authors. I am confident that the book will be of great service to
teachers and students in the physical laboratory.—Harry C. Jones, Ph.D.,
Instructor in Physical Chemistry, Johns Hopkins University.

NEW YORK AND LONDON
HARPER & BROTHERS, PUBLISHERS

Milton Keynes UK
Ingram Content Group UK Ltd.
UKHW051809101023
430259UK00020B/170